Please Don't Eat the Daisies

by Jean Kerr

Drawings by
Martha Blanchard

FAWCETT CREST • NEW YORK

For my severest critic

CONTENTS

		PAGE
	Introduction	11
1.	*Please don't eat the daisies*	21
2.	*How to be a collector's item*	27
3.	*Greenwich, anyone?*	35
4.	*How to decorate in one easy breakdown*	41
5.	*Dogs that have known me*	51
6.	*The Kerr-Hilton*	57
7.	*The care and feeding of producers*	73
8.	*One half of two on the aisle*	81
9.	*Don Brown's body*	89
10.	*Toujours tristesse*	101

11. *Snowflaketime*   107

12. *How to get the best of your children*   113

13. *Where did you put the aspirin?*   119

14. *Aunt Jean's marshmallow fudge diet*   127

15. *Operation operation*   135

Please Don't
Eat the Daisies

Introduction

I HAD THE FEELING all along that this book should have an Introduction, because it doesn't have an Index and it ought to have *something*. But I was getting nowhere until I received this dandy questionnaire from the publicity department at Doubleday.

Now, I'm an old hand at questionnaires, having successfully opened a charge account at The Tailored Woman. But this was a questionnaire with a difference. It had heart. Take the item: Why do you write? In less artful hands this might have been a touchy question, indicating—perhaps—a last-minute case of nerves at the head office. Instead, one felt that they cared. They just wanted to *know*, that's all.

Of course, there were a certain number of routine questions. List your pen name. (I just call it Ball-Point.) What do you do when you're not writing? (Buy geraniums.) Husband's name? (Honey.) List your previous addresses.(Funny, that's what The Tailored Woman was so curious about.)

But then we began to probe deeper. What is your life's ambition? What do you hope to accomplish ere

11

I had the feeling all along that this book
should have an introduction . . .

dusk sets in? As far as this book is concerned, who should be notified in case of accident?

It was this next to last question that really yanked me to attention. It made me realize—and for the very first time—that in my scant two score minus seven years (all right, I'm the same age as Margaret Truman; let somebody check on *her*) I have already *achieved* my life ambition. That's something, you know. I feel it sets me apart, rather, like that nice convict who raises canaries in San Quentin.

To go back to the beginning, I was only eight years old, and clearly retarded for my age, when my goal in life dawned on me. I won't say there was a blinding flash, just a poignance, a suspension of time, a sweet recognition of the moment of truth not unlike that memorable instant in which Johnny Weissmuller first noticed that he was Tarzan and *not* Jane.

It was seven-thirty in the morning and my sister, who was six, was pulling my feet out from under the bedclothes and crying, "Oh, get up, get *up*, you mean thing, Mother says I can't go downstairs until you're on the floor!" I withered her with one of my characteristically salty sayings—"Oh, you think you're so smart, Lady Jane Grey!"—but as I stumbled out of bed I realized then and there that all I wanted out of life was to be able to sleep until noon. In fact, I composed a poem right on the spot to celebrate the discovery. I remember the poem (unfortunately reprinted here in its entirety) because it is the only one I ever wrote, unless you want to include a two-line Valentine which said "Thee—whee." The poem:

Dearer to me than the evening star
A Packard car.
A Hershey bar
Or a bride in her rich adorning
Dearer than any of these by far
Is to lie in bed in the morning.

Of course I realized even then that you can't sleep until noon with the proper élan unless you have some legitimate reason for staying up until three (parties don't count). But I was in high school before I grasped the fact that *I* was never going to do anything that would keep me up until three. I had been writing short stories which, in the first flush of failure, I sent to *Liberty Magazine* on the innocent but quite mistaken theory that *Liberty* would buy them because everything in the magazine was so terrible. (The only story I can remember now was called "The Pursuit of Happiness" and I wince to report that Happiness was the heroine's name.)

The solution, for me, was obvious: I had to locate a husband who stayed up until three. With this in mind, I ruled out basketball players, who were the natural objects of my affection at the time (I was five feet nine). It had been my observation that all basketball players eventually joined their fathers in the construction business, an activity notorious for its chaste and early uprisings. Besides, I didn't want to marry a basketball player anyway. I really wanted to marry George S. Kaufman and was deterred only by the fact that (a) he had a wife, and (b) I never met him.

It may not seem very romantic, and I don't think Victor Herbert could have done a thing with it, but by the time I was eighteen Walter (my husband) was the only truly eligible man I had ever met. He was an assistant professor who began teaching his classes at three in the afternoon and who directed plays all night. Actually, he got up at *ten* o'clock in the morning, but that was close enough. It was something to build on. And, to be entirely fair, he had certain other endearing qualities. He could play "Ja-Da" on the piano, recite whole sections of *The Waste Land* and make passable penuche. So we were married and I began each day bright and late at the stroke of the noon whistle, a splendid state of affairs which continued for two years or right up to the moment our first son was born.

Now the thing about having a baby—and I can't be the first person to have noticed this—is that thereafter you *have* it, and it's years before you can distract it from any elemental need by saying, "Oh, for heaven's sake, go look at television." At this point I was willing to renounce my master plan—so doth parenthood make cowards of us all—and go to bed at a decent hour like everybody else. Unfortunately, Walter was still staying up until three, busily engaged in making student actors look older by the ingenious device of keeping the stage lights very dim, and I was seeing *him* during the late hours, the children during the early hours, and double all the rest of the time.

It took me quite a while to come to grips with the situation, basically because I was thinking so slowly (from the lack of sleep) and because I had to spend so much time trying to remember to turn off the sterilized nipples before they melted. Eventually, after several years and several children, it came to me that the solution was to hire somebody *else* to get up in the morning.

At the university, we lived basically on a teacher's salary, which is the way you live on a teacher's salary; and this meant that if we were going to have a helpmate, I, Mommy, would have to make some money to pay her. But how? A job was out of the question: getting up in the morning was what I was trying to avoid. It had to be something I could do at home among the cans of Dextri-Maltose. But what? Could I sell little batches of my own special chicken creole soup, which I make by mixing together one can of Campbell's chicken soup with one can of Campbell's creole soup? No.

So I decided to write plays, spurred on by a chance compliment my father had paid me years earlier. "Look," he exploded one evening over the dinner table, "the only damn thing in this world you're good for is *talk*." By talk I assumed he meant dialogue—and I was off.

I won't say that my early efforts were crowned with glory. Oh, I'd say it, all right, but could I make it stick? When my first play was produced in New York, Louis Kronenberger wrote in *Time*, with a felicity it took me only ten years to appreciate, that "Leo G. Carroll brightens up Mrs. Kerr's play in much the same way that flowers brighten a sickroom." (I guess this is what they mean by the nick of *Time*.) I don't know why this and similar compliments for Leo G. Carroll didn't stay my hand forever. As someone pointed out recently, if you can keep your head when all about you are losing theirs, it's just possible you haven't grasped the situation. But what with one thing and another (the advance paid by the doomed producer, and the amateur rights) I was now paying the salary of a very nice girl who had insomnia anyway and who pretended to enjoy distributing pablum and crayons until I emerged, rosy and wrinkled, at eleven in the morning.

Thus, as the golden years rolled on, I typed my way through several maids. There was a brief, ghastly period, immediately after we left the university, when it looked as though Walter was going to take a civilian-type job and we might have to live, oh think of it, *normally*. But my fears were groundless and Walter became a drama critic. In many ways, a drama critic leads an ideal existence, or would if he didn't have to see so many plays.

Obviously, it's fun to share the opening-night excitement of a great big hit. And there are, every year, a certain number of plays that must be labeled failures (because they close, for one thing) which are nevertheless fascinating to watch. But then, alas, there are the dogs (the worst of these usually turn up in March or April, which is the origin of the phrase "the hounds of spring"). These are the plays that are so bad you sit there in stunned disbelief, fearing for your sanity while on all sides people are beating their way to the exits. It was after just such an evening that my husband commented, "This is the kind of play that gives failures a bad name."

I don't know what set of standards the critics themselves bring to these occasions. But *I* can sense the presence of a real disaster, where no one will be allowed to enter the area for twenty-four hours, by gauging the amount of incidental information I've picked up about the bit players. We sit so far front that it is possible to read by the light-spill from the stage. And through the years I have discovered that on a really grueling evening it helps to keep me alert—that is to say, *conscious*—if I study the program notes while the performance is going on. "Biff Nuthall," I read, "Here making his debut in New York in the part of the elevator boy, hails from Princeton, New Jersey. He attended the University of Wisconsin, where he achieved notable success as Mosca in a student production of *Volpone*. Mr. Nuthall also plays the oboe."

As you can see, I now have something to chew over; my subconscious is now gainfully occupied. Biff Nuthall as Mosca. I'm sure that boy is loaded with talent, but he'd never be *my* idea of Mosca. Benvolio maybe, or Friar Laurence; but Mosca—with those freckles and that red hair? And if he hails from Princeton, New Jersey, what was he doing going to the University of Wisconsin? What's the matter with Princeton, for heaven's sake? But that's the way some boys are: just because a college is located in their home town, it's not good enough for them. I'm sure you had your reasons, Biff, but it doesn't seem loyal, somehow. And another thing: what do they mean by that curt statement: "Mr. Nuthall also plays the oboe"? Do I imagine it, or is there a rebuke implied there somewhere? Doesn't he play it very well? Or does the press agent, who composed this little biography, not have a very high opinion of the oboe? For his information, the oboe is a noble instrument too much neglected by young people nowadays. What does he want, an entire orchestra composed of violins?

If the cast is long enough, one can while away a whole evening in this manner.

I do have a compulsion to read in out-of-the-way places, and it is often a blessing; on the other hand, it sometimes comes between me and what I tell the children is *"my* work." As a matter of fact, I will read *anything* rather than work. And I don't mean interesting things like the yellow section of the telephone book or the enclosures that come with the Bloomingdale bill about McKettrick classics in sizes 12 to 20, blue, brown, or navy @ 12.95 (by the way, did you know that colored facial tissue is now on sale at the unbelievably low price of 7.85 a carton?). The truth is that, rather than put a word on paper, I will spend a whole half hour reading the label on a milk-of-magnesia bottle. "Philips' Milk of Magnesia," I read with the absolute absorption of someone just stumbling on Congreve, "is prepared only by the Charles H. Philips Co., division of Sterling Drug, Inc. Not to be used when abdominal pain, nausea, vomiting, or other symptoms of appendicitis are present, etc."

For this reason, and because I have four boys, I do about half of my "work" in the family car, parked alongside a sign that says "Littering Is Punishable by a $50 Fine." So far as the boys are concerned it's not the direct interruptions at home that are hard to adjust to. I don't mind when one of them rushes in to tell me something really important, like the Good Humor man said that banana-rum was going to be the flavor of the week next week. What really drives me frantic and leads to the use of such quantities of Tint-Hair is the business of overhearing a chance remark from another part of the house ("Listen, stupid, the water is supposed to go in the *top*"). Rather than investigate, and interrupt myself, I spend twenty minutes wondering: What water? The top of what? I hope it's just a water gun and not, oh no, not the enema bag again.

Out in the car, where I freeze to death or roast to

death depending on the season, all is serene. The few things there are to read in the front-seat area (Chevrolet, E-gasoline-F, 100-temp-200) I have long since committed to memory. So there is nothing to do but write, after I have the glove compartment tidied up.

Once in a while—perhaps every fifteen minutes or so—I ask myself: Why do I struggle, when I could be home painting the kitchen cupboards, *why?* And then I remember. Because I like to sleep in the morning, that's why.

1. Please don't eat the daisies

WE ARE BEING very careful with our children. They'll never have to pay a psychiatrist twenty-five dollars an hour to find out why we rejected them. We'll tell them why we rejected them. Because they're impossible, that's why.

It seems to me, looking back on it, that everything was all right when there were two of them and two of us. We felt loved, protected, secure. But now that there are four of them and two of us, things have changed. We're in the minority, we're not as vigorous as we used to be, and it's clear that we cannot compete with these younger men.

You take Christopher—and you *may;* he's a slightly used eight-year-old. The source of our difficulty with him lies in the fact that he is interested in the precise value of words whereas we are only interested in having him pick his clothes up off the floor. I say, "Christopher, you take a bath and put all your things in the wash," and he says, "Okay, but it will break the Bendix." Now at this point the shrewd rejoinder would be, "That's all right, let it break the Bendix." But years of experience have washed over me in vain and I, perennial patsy, inquire, "*Why* will it break the Bendix?" So he explains, "Well, if I put *all* my things in the wash, I'll have to put my shoes in and they will certainly break the machinery."

21

They'll never have to pay a psychiatrist
twenty-five dollars an hour . . .

"Very well," I say, all sweetness and control, "put everything but the shoes in the wash." He picks up my agreeable tone at once, announcing cheerily, "Then you *do* want me to put my belt in the wash." I don't know what I say at this point, but my husband says, "Honey, you mustn't scream at him that way."

Another version of this battle of semantics would be:

"Don't kick the table leg with your foot."

"I'm not kicking, I'm tapping."

"Well, don't tap with your foot."

"It's not my foot, it's a fork."

"Well, don't tap with the fork."

"It's not a *good* fork" . . . et cetera, et cetera.

Christopher is an unusual child in other respects. I watch him from the kitchen window. With a garden rake in one hand he scampers up a tree, out across a long branch, and down over the stone wall—as graceful and as deft as a squirrel. On the other hand, he is unable to get from the living room into the front hall without bumping into at least two pieces of furniture. (I've seen him hit as many as five, but that's championship stuff and he can't do it every time.)

He has another trick which defies analysis, and also the laws of gravity. He can walk out into the middle of a perfectly empty kitchen and trip on the linoleum. I *guess* it's the linoleum. There isn't anything else there.

My friends who have children are always reporting the quaint and agreeable utterances of their little ones. For example, the mother of one five-year-old philosopher told me that when she appeared at breakfast in a new six-dollar pink wrap-around, her little boy chirped, in a tone giddy with wonder, "Oh, look, our Miss Mommy must be going to a wedding!" Now I don't think any one of my children would say a thing like that. (What do I mean I don't *think;* there are some things about which you can be positive.) Of course, in a six-dollar wrap-around I wouldn't look as if I were going to a wedding. I'd look as if I were going to paint the garage. But that's not the point. The point is: where is that babbling, idiotic loyalty that other mothers get?

A while back I spoke of a time when there were two of them and two of us. In my affinity for round numbers I'm falsifying the whole picture. Actually, there never were two of them. There was one of them, and all of a sudden there were three of them.

The twins are four now, and for several years we have had galvanized iron fencing lashed onto the outside of their bedroom windows. This gives the front of the house a rather institutional look and contributes to unnecessary rumors about my mental health, but it does keep them off the roof, which is what we had in mind.

For twins they are very dissimilar. Colin is tall and active and Johnny is short and middle-aged. Johnny doesn't kick off his shoes, he doesn't swallow beer caps or tear pages out of the telephone book. I don't think he ever draws pictures with my best lipstick. In fact, he has none of the charming, lighthearted "boy" qualities that precipitate so many scenes of violence in the home. On the other hand, he has a feeling for order and a passion for system that would be trying in a head nurse. If his pajamas are hung on the third hook in the closet instead of on the second hook, it causes him real pain. If one slat in a Venetian blind is tipped in the wrong direction he can't have a moment's peace until somebody fixes it. Indeed, if one of the beans on his plate is slightly longer than the others he can scarcely bear to eat it. It's hard for him to live with the rest of us. And vice versa.

Colin is completely different. He has a lightness of touch and a dexterity that will certainly put him on top of the heap if he ever takes up safe-cracking. Equipped with only a spoon and an old emery board, he can take a door off its hinges in seven minutes and remove all of the towel racks from the bathroom in five.

. . . I'm going to a psychiatrist and find out why I have this feeling of persecution . . . this sense of being continually surrounded . . .

Gilbert is only seventeen months old, and it's too early to tell about him. (As a matter of fact, we can tell, all right, but we're just not ready to face it.) Once upon a time we might have been taken in by smiles and gurgles and round blue eyes, but no more. We know he is just biding his time. Today he can't do much more than eat his shoelaces and suck off an occasional button. Tomorrow, the world.

My real problem with children is that I haven't any imagination. I'm always warning them against the commonplace defections while they are planning the bizarre and unusual. Christopher gets up ahead of the rest of us on Sunday mornings and he has long since been given a list of clear directives: "Don't wake the baby," "Don't go outside in your pajamas," "Don't eat cookies before breakfast." But I never told him, "Don't make flour paste and glue together all the pages of the magazine section of the Sunday *Times*." Now I tell him, of course.

And then last week I had a dinner party and told the twins and Christopher not to go in the living room, not to use the guest towels in the bathroom, and not to leave the bicycles on the front steps. However, I neglected to tell them not to eat the daisies on the dining-room table. This was a serious omission, as I discovered when I came upon my centerpiece—a charming three-point arrangement of green stems.

The thing is, I'm going to a psychiatrist and find out why I have this feeling of persecution . . . this sense of being continually surrounded. . . .

2. *How to be a collector's item*

I WAS READING another volume of collected letters last night, and it sent me right back to worrying about that old problem. On what basis do you decide that your friends are going to be famous, and that you ought to be saving their letters? Naturally, you save everything you get from Ernest Hemingway and Edith Sitwell. But think of the smart boys who were saving Edna Millay's penciled notes when she was just a slip of a thing at Vassar. What gets me is how they *knew*.

As sure as you're born, I'm tossing stuff into the wastebasket this minute that Scribner's would give their eyeteeth for twenty years from now. But you can't save *everybody's* letters, not in that five-room apartment. When I was young and naïve, last year, I used to file away mail if it seemed interesting or amusing. But that was a trap. For instance, I have a marvelous letter from my cleaning man explaining how he happened to break the coffee table. But clearly this is a one-shot affair. *He'll* never be collected. You have to use a little sense about these things.

No doubt the safest procedure is to confine yourself to those friends who have demonstrated a marked literary bent. Even then, I wouldn't collect anybody who didn't seem a good risk. If you have a friend who is a novelist, you might play it very close to the ground and wait until he wins a Pulitzer prize. Of course, by that time he may not be writing to *you* any more. His correspondence will very likely be limited to letters to the Columbia Broadcasting System explaining why it isn't convenient for him to appear on *Person to Person*.

If you have a friend who is a playwright, it's simpler. You begin collecting *him* immediately after his first failure. As letter writers, playwrights are at the top of their powers at this moment. For color, passion, and direct revelation of character you simply can't beat a letter from a playwright who has just had a four-day flop.

And sometimes you can see a talent bloom before your very eyes. I have one friend, a poet, who used to write nice little things about "the icy fingers of November" and "the strange stillnesss of ash trays after a party." I admit I didn't take him very seriously. But just last week he had a long poem in the *Partisan Review* and I didn't understand one word of it. Well, let me tell you, I'm saving his letters *now*.

You've got to keep your wits about you. It would be terrible to think you were brushing with greatness and didn't even notice. Oh, I'll admit there are times when you just can't be certain whether or not a friend has talent. In that case, just ask him. He'll tell you. But here, too, some discretion is necessary. For example, I don't give any serious attention to friends who get drunk at cocktail parties and announce they could write a better book than *Marjorie Morningstar*.

On the whole, I'd say that if you have a very promising circle of acquaintances who appear regularly in the newspapers announcing that their beer is Rheingold the dry beer and on the networks pouring out their little secrets to Tex and Jinx, your path as a collector is clear. Leave town. Otherwise, they won't have any opportunity to write to you.

But who am I trying to fool with all this nonsense? Obviously, I'm not really worrying about my friends' letters. What keeps me awake nights is the question of

my letters, the ones *I* write. Are they being saved?
Fat chance. I know my friends—it simply wouldn't
enter their scatterbrained heads that they ought to be
collecting me. And poor Doubleday, how will they ever
scrape together a book? Well, they won't, that's all, if
I don't take steps. . .

So I'm taking steps. From now on I keep carbons of
every word I write, and to hell with my cavalier pen-
pals. I've got a very decent sampling already:

Dear Mabel,
    Johnny doesn't seem to have a pair of socks
without holes so tell him he has to wear one
brown sock and one green sock. If he makes
a fuss—tell him he can wear his long pants
and they won't show. And another thing, very
important—it's Gilbert's turn to drink his
milk out of the beer mug.

                                        Mrs. K.

Joan, dear—
    Well, we finally moved into Hilltop and
what a magical place it is! High, high
above the slate-blue waters of the Bay.
We have our very own special, sad, sighing wind.
It seems enchanted and, we fancy, it is full
of ghosts of Heathcliff and his Catherine.
Promise you'll come and see us. We're always
here.

                                        Love,
                                            Jean

The All-Season Window Corp.,
Mount Vernon, N. Y.
Dear Sirs,
    Listen, are you going to come and put in
those storm windows before we are blown out
into the damn Sound? You said Monday and

From now on, I keep carbons of every word I write . . .

here it is Wednesday. We keep the thermostat
up to eighty-five and still the toast is flying
off the plates. And I had to put mittens
on to type this.

I hope to hear from you soon or never.

Jean Kerr

Dear Phyllis,

Thank you, thank you, thank you—for an
evening of pure bliss. Your book arrived
yesterday morning and it hasn't been out of
my hands since. Much have I traveled in
realms of gold—but truly, Phyllis, this
is a coup. It *needed* to be said. As Sainte-
Beuve once remarked, *"Je ne sais quois pour
dire."*

Gratefully,
J.

Mother darling,

I'm sorry I didn't write to you for the
last three weeks but we were picking out
our Christmas card. I think your slogan
for the Runyon Cancer Fund is excellent. I
would by all means mail it in to the contest.
Not much new here except that for some reason
Joan dropped in yesterday with her four horrible
children—three of whom had harmonicas. Oh,
and did you read Phyllis' book? Yap, yap, yap
over the same material. She seems to think she
owns the seventeenth century. No, I haven't
seen Tab Hunter in *Battle Cry*, but if you say
it's a "must" I'll have to catch it.

Love and kisses, J.

Treasurer,
Hellinger Theatre,
New York, N. Y.

Dear Sir,

What do you mean by returning my check and
saying there are no seats available for *My
Fair Lady?* I asked for two good seats on
the first available Wednesday evening. Do
you mean to suggest that down through the
echoing corridors of time there will *never*
be a Wednesday night on which two seats will
be available? I don't wish to inject an empty
note of pessimism but even you, in the first
flush and fever of success, must concede that
there is a possibility—at least in theory—
that sometime, say in 1962, you might be willing,
even anxious, to sell two seats.

In the meantime, I'm going to see *Bells Are
Ringing.*

                                    Outraged

Honey,

I seem to have lost my car key in Schrafft's
so will you please take a cab and go pick up
the car which I left in front of Bloomingdale's
in New Rochelle? It's in a no-parking area but
I don't think that matters because it's raining
and Peggy says they never check in the rain.
There are a lot of groceries on the back seat
and I don't know what you're going to do with
the ice cream.

                                    Love, J.

Funnell's Market,

Dear Sirs,

Enclosed you will find a check for my
February bill. However, I wish to draw
your attention to one item which reads
"Fifty cents' worth of spiced ham @ 70
cents." I am aware of rising cost and
the resultant strain on independent grocers,
but nevertheless when I order fifty cents' worth
of spiced ham I expect to get it @ .50.

> Yours cordially,
> Jean Kerr

Dear Chris,

Daddy and I are going out to supper and I
want you to pay attention to this list.
1. No Disneyland until your homework is done.
2. Get your bicycle and all those guns out
of the bathroom.
3. Take a bath and be sure to put one cup
of Tide in the water.
4. Don't wear your underwear or your socks
to bed.
5. Col says you swallowed his whistle. If
you didn't, give it back to him.

> Love, Mommy

Mr. Ken McCormick,
Doubleday & Co.,
New York, N. Y.

Dear Ken,

Thank you for saying the letters were in-

teresting, and I shall, as you suggest, try
Random House.

As always,
Jean

P.S.: Will you kindly return this letter?

3. Greenwich, anyone?

THE THING that worries me is that I am so different from other writers. Connecticut is just another state to me. And nature—well, nature is just nature. When I see a tree whose leafy mouth is pressed against the earth's sweet flowing breast, I think, "Well, *that's* a nice-looking oak," but it doesn't change my way of life.

Now I'm not going to stand here and run down trees and flowers. Personally, I have three snake plants of my own, and in a tearoom I'm the first one to notice the geraniums. But the point is, I keep my head.

However, I've been reading a lot lately, and it's clear that I'm out of step. Most serious writers of stature (I consider a writer serious when he makes more than twenty thousand a year) are giving up their psychiatrists and going back to the land. You can't pick up a book these days without getting all involved with the inspirational saga of some poor, harried writer who was making sixty thousand a year and taking the five fifty-one back to Larchmont, but it was all ashes—ashes.

Then he found this old abandoned sawmill in Connecticut that was three hours from the station and twenty minutes from the bathroom, and there he found contentment.

Right from the beginning the golden days were flow-

ing to the brim with the real stuff of life and living. No
matter that the maid quit because she wasn't used to
cooking over an open hearth. As soon as the wife opened
a can of Heinz's spaghetti, sprinkled it with marjoram,
chervil, anise, and some dry vermouth, she once again
felt the sweet fulfillment of being a mate and a mother.
The children were no problem, because they had to walk
eight miles back and forth to school and were scarcely
ever around.

And Truth itself came knocking one morning, along
about ten-fifteen. It was a pretty spring day, the but-
tercups were twinkling on the grass, and the only
sound was the song of the whippoorwill until the chim-
ney broke off and fell down through the dining-room
ceiling, scattering beams, bricks, and mortar here and
there and quite demolishing the French Provincial
table.

Our writer came upon the wreckage on his way back
from the well. Although he was dismayed at first, he
took hold of himself and did what anyone else would
have done in the situation. He went out and sat on the
back stoop. Pretty soon a chicken came strolling by. He
picked it up, and suddenly he became aware that it
was warm and that it was making little cheeping
sounds and that it was *his* chicken. He held it against
his last clean shirt. Now he was lost, lost in the mir-
acle of the warmth and the scratching and cheeping—
even though, as I understand it, cheeping is not at all
unusual in chickens. Forgotten was the hole in the roof,
forgotten the dining-room table. He realized that nothing
else really mattered: from now on it was going to be him
and this chicken.

Well, you see how different we all are. I simply can't
think of a household disaster that would be in any way
mitigated by the presence of a chicken in the back
yard. And on the day the roof fell in, a smart chicken
would keep out of my way. At a time like that, it would

... it was *his* chicken.

be nothing for me to go out and kick one in the tail feathers. But then I hate chickens, with their blank beady eyes and the silly way they keep shaking their scrawny little heads.

Formerly, when our writer lived in the sinful city, five o'clock was a nightmare of cocktail parties at which he could never get a martini that was dry enough (his own method with martinis seems to have consisted in keeping the gin locked away in a separate closet and walking past it once a week carrying a bottle of vermouth). Now five o'clock finds him up to his elbows in cows. "The Boy and I finished the milking, and there, in sight of the cows, we sat down with a pail of the rich, warm brew and refreshed ourselves." Of course, he may only mean that they washed themselves in it, but doesn't it sound like they *drank* it?

Then he adds, "My, how The Boy is shooting up. He is already an inch taller than The Girl." I don't know what gets into writers when they move to the country. They can't remember the names of their children. Two weeks in the dew-soaked fields, and the best they can do is The Boy and The Girl. Notice, though, the way they keep tabs on the livestock. You're always reading how "Lord Peter Wimsey got a nail in his hoof today," or "Thank heaven, Edith Sitwell finally had her kittens."

All is not work, work, work in Utopia. Oftentimes, in the evening after they have finished spreading the fertilizer, the writer and his wife sit on the fence—with a wonderful sense of "togetherness"—and listen to the magic symphony of the crickets. I can understand that. Around our house we're pretty busy, and of course we're not the least bit integrated, but nevertheless my husband and I often sit together in the deepening twilight and listen to the sweet, gentle slosh-click, slosh-click of the dishwasher. He smiles and I smile. Oh, it's a golden moment.

But to get back to the writer. Even from his standpoint, there is one tiny flaw in all this bucolic bliss.

What with setting the winter potatoes and keeping the cows freshened, he hasn't done a lick of writing since he got there. Of course, he *has* kept a diary—and this becomes our only means of studying the effects of contentment on a writer's style. The effects are awesome.

Here was our boy, writing lovely, depressing stories for the more advanced magazines. (I remember a typical one about a stout woman of fifty with an Italian haircut, who got very drunk in a club car and proceeded to tell a lot of perfect strangers why she wouldn't give Harry a divorce.) *Now* listen to him:

"Up at five-thirty to help with the lambing.

"Saw a yellow-bellied snipwhistle.

"Oh, such excitement as there was today. The corn shucker arrived."

Help with a lambing at five-thirty? That settles it. I won't *be* a writer.

4. How to decorate in one easy breakdown

As a RESULT of a recent impartial survey taken among the ladies at one table in Stouffer's, I have discovered a number of significant facts about home decorating that I am perfectly willing to share.

The problem confronting the average harassed housewife today is not whether she's going to decorate. Of course she's going to decorate. The problem is *when.* I find that circumstances vary, but in general it is safe to list three situations in which it is advisable to redo the living room: (1) when you have the money; (2) when you don't have the money but are planning to go on *The $64,000 Question,* where you will astonish all with your knowledge of rare bindings; (3) when you don't have the money and there's not a chance in the world you're going to get the money, but if you have to look at that speckled blue wallpaper one more day you will go smack out of your mind.

Having decided that you are going to go ahead with the project, you come up against the really ticklish question of *how*—in what color, in what style—you are going to do the room. It is at this point that many stout hearts decide to stay with speckled blue wallpaper. For it is a curious fact that even those women who ordinarily intimidate their closest friends by the instant and absolute conviction they bring to all sub-

41

. . . one more day you will go smack out of your mind.

jects suddenly develop vast areas of insecurity the moment they have to say whether the ceiling should be painted lighter or darker than the walls.

I know one woman of unusually strong character who selected a college for her son in a single afternoon and who has always been able to plan a dinner for sixteen in five minutes. In a beauty parlor, when the manicurist asks her what color she wants her nails, she can glance at a rack of nineteen bottles of nail polish and announce "Carioca Pink" without a second's hesitation.

She is, as I say, exceptional. I was all the more surprised, then, to meet her in Schumacher's last week on what was her seventh visit to that establishment for the purpose of selecting an upholstery fabric for one wing chair. Gone was that brave air of decision and dispatch. Before me, adrift in a sea of samples, sat a broken figure pathetically waving swatches of damask and asking advice from total strangers.

To avoid this sort of thing it is helpful to get the advice of a decorator. There is, in fact, nothing in the world like a good, first-rate professional decorator to convince a normal woman that she knows exactly what she wants to do with her own living room. The decorator invariably arrives with a notebook and an air of chilly preoccupation. He tiptoes cautiously around That Tragic Error, your living room, and finally flashes a sudden, sympathetic smile that seems to say, "Thank God you called me. Another month and it might have been too late."

Then he speaks: "My dear, you have a small, dark room with very poor fenestration. I see pale, silver ash." And you say, "What do you mean, pale, silver ash—*gray?* It *is* gray. It's been gray for fifteen years." You nerve yourself. "I thought turquoise—with maybe a touch of pink."

At the mention of the word "turquoise" a look of such pain washes over his face as to suggest that he is suffering a sudden gall-bladder attack. When he has pulled himself together he speaks quietly and with great patience: "But my dear lady, you *do* want a room that is outgoing?" "Yes, yes," you say, "of course—naturally—I want a room that's outgoing, but couldn't it also be something—well, different?"

He dismisses this question with the contempt it deserves and marches over to your small, charming fireplace. He taps it with his pencil. "Victorian, of course." "Oh, yes," you burble helpfully, "it is perfect Victorian. That fireplace is really the reason we bought this house in the first place." "Well"—"Well"—his manner is now brisk and to the point—"we won't have any trouble with that. We can just rip it out and put in sheetrock." And it's right here you decide that what's going to be outgoing in this room is that decorator.

At this juncture you may be tempted to ask your husband for advice. Don't. Husbands as a class have two different approaches to home decoration. First, there is the constructive but useless attitude: "Blue is such a pretty color, why don't you make everything blue?" Then there is the destructive but useless attitude: "Oh, do what you want, but for Heaven's sake, don't have a lot of bloodshot petunias hanging all over the place like your sister Helen."

With such a man there is no point in explaining that those petunias are, in fact, carnations and that they repose on a hand-screened English linen that costs $18.75 a yard.

You might look for help in the tonier magazines, although the pretty people in those four-color layouts don't seem to live like the rest of us. In the first place, they apparently spend all their time out on terraces or patios where they are photographed reclining in redwood chairs or chastely broiling filets over expensive braziers. This outdoor life is undoubtedly sensible. How else would they get the strength and vigor nec-

... What's going to be outgoing in this room
is that decorator.

essary for springing out of that curious low furniture they keep in the living room?

I do realize that most people nowadays—certainly all people of taste and distinction—live in ranch-type houses with three glass walls and one brick wall and a huge green plant where the fireplace should be. But wouldn't you think that some adventurous magazine would give an occasional nod to the few stragglers in every community who still live in ordinary houses with porches and pillars and dining rooms and things like that?

Once in a while you do see a picture of an attractive traditional room. Just last month I came across a room done entirely in sea-foam green and chalk white. The only color accents were one red apple and a bright red magazine on the coffee table. It was lovely. Of course, you would have to be continually replacing that apple, and down through the years somebody would be bound to inquire why you were still hanging onto that 1935 copy of *Charm*. Then there are those "How To" pieces. I read a splendid one some time ago entitled "There Are Treasures in Your Attic." It was accompanied by a tantalizing series of pictures which demonstrated how a number of enterprising women had transformed forgotten monstrosities—dilapidated furniture, old nail kegs, that sort of thing—into "Conversation Pieces."

One canny lady rescued a battered dresser belonging to her great-grandfather and hacked it into three sections. The bottom section she covered with plywood and parchment paper to make a very quaint coffee table ("quaint" was the word *they* used). The middle piece, after it had been sanded and pickled and equipped with cunning little brass handles, became a night table. And the top section, a drawer with a mirror over it, was sanded and stained and hung in the entrance hall.

In this way she had *three* conversation pieces. She may even have gone too far. As I see it, when this giddy carpenter has guests to the house they never will get around to the important topics—like the weather or the Dodgers. They'll spend the whole long night talking about the furniture.

Anyway, after I'd finished the article I was so filled with guilt at the thought of the marvels lying fallow above me that I sprained my ankle racing up to the attic. What I found there was one file cabinet and an infant's crib. If I'd had two file cabinets I might have painted them with the radiator paint, trimmed them with decals, placed them side by side and I'd have had a small but adorable breakfront. However, I defy *House and Garden* or anybody else to do anything with an infant's crib except put an infant in it.

To get back to those old nail kegs. Did you know that, properly treated, they'd make a charming pair of end tables for a rumpus room? If, for one reason or another, you shouldn't happen to have any old nail kegs in your attic, you can buy them—with the nails—for $19.50 apiece, which is only a little more than you'd pay for an ordinary end table and then, of course, you'll have all those nails.

Unquestionably, some people do have more imagination than others. A friend of mine, for instance, owned an old bed with huge hand-carved posts. She sawed off one of the posts, had it wired, and bought an expensive raw silk lampshade for it. This *was* a conversation piece. All of her friends commented on it. They said, "Good Lord, Peggy, isn't that a bedpost and aren't you even going to paint it or something?"

It does no good, incidentally, to pour out your decorating problems to your friends. They always respond with some practical suggestion like "If I were you, Grace, I'd leave it just the way it is until the children are grown."

As a matter of fact, a neighbor of mine took this piece of advice. She waited until the children were grown

and married, and then she invested in her heart's desire
—a new white rug beneath salmon-pink hangings. I
was over there the other day. On the new white rug
beneath the salmon-pink hangings she was entertain-
ing her five grandchildren, their boxer dog, and four
turtles.

But we are digressing. Even if you are going to re-do
your living room, you'll probably have to put up with
most of the furniture you already have, including that
sturdy sofa you bought in 1923, the month after the twins
were born. Therefore, it will be mostly a matter of slipcovers, drapes, and paint.

When you go to pick out fabrics, it is sometimes
easier to go to a large department store where nobody
will ever wait on you. This way you are left alone for
hours to mull over rolls and rolls of fabric. In a regu-
lar fabric house you get such excellent and individual
attention that it is practically impossible to make a
selection.

Whereas you just want to prowl around and look
and be left alone with your samples and your memories, they want to *help* you. By the time the salesman
has graciously and tenderly arranged twenty-eight
samples on the austere rack in front of your arm-
chair, you begin to get a feeling of mounting panic
that you are *never* going to like anything and that
this lovely man is going to know you for the failure
you are.

In this situation, I find it very helpful to divert the
salesman. I usually say, "Yes, it's lovely, lovely—but
—I have to consider how it will go with my pink grand
piano."

The salesman is now definitely diverted. In fact, he is
shaken to his foundations. In a moment or so he will
be suggesting, in a strained voice, "Lady, the racks
are over there—why don't you just look?" And you
do go look, while he takes up a watchful post near the
telephone, ready to summon help at a moment's notice.

In due time you will have selected material for your

slipcovers, picked out a darker color for the drapes and a lighter color for the walls, and dropped the whole confusing assortment at an upholsterer's. One day seven months later everything arrives, and it's beautiful, beautiful—or maybe it isn't. You can always do it over again in eighteen or nineteen years.

5. Dogs that have known me

I NEVER MEANT to say anything about this, but the fact is that I have never met a dog that didn't have it in for me. You take Kelly, for instance. He's a wire-haired fox terrier and he's had us for three years now. I wouldn't say that he was terribly handsome but he does have a very nice smile. What he *doesn't* have is any sense of fitness. All the other dogs in the neighborhood spend their afternoons yapping at each other's heels or chasing cats. Kelly spends his whole day, every day, chasing swans on the millpond. I don't actually worry because he will never catch one. For one thing, he can't swim. Instead of settling for a simple dog-paddle like everybody else, he has to show off and try some complicated overhand stroke, with the result that he always sinks and has to be fished out. Naturally, people talk, and I never take him for a walk that somebody doesn't point him out and say, "There's that crazy dog that chases swans."

Another thing about that dog is that he absolutely refuses to put himself in the other fellow's position. We have a pencil sharpener in the kitchen and Kelly used to enjoy having an occasional munch on the plastic cover. As long as it was just a nip now and then, I didn't mind. But one day he simply lost his head and ate the whole thing. Then I had to buy a new one

and of course I put it up high out of Kelly's reach.
Well, the scenes we were treated to—and the sulking!
In fact, ever since he has been eating things I know he
doesn't like just to get even. I don't mean things like
socks and mittens and paper napkins, which of course
are delicious. Lately he's been eating plastic airplanes,
suede brushes, and light bulbs. Well, if he wants to sit
under the piano and make low and loving growls over
a suede brush just to show me, okay. But frankly I think
he's lowering himself.

Time and again I have pointed out to Kelly that with
discriminating dogs, dogs who are looking for a finer,
lighter chew—it's bedroom slippers two to one. I have
even dropped old, dilapidated bedroom slippers here and
there behind the furniture, hoping to tempt him. But
the fact is, that dog wouldn't touch a bedroom slipper
if he was starving.

Although we knew that, as a gourmet, he was a wash-
out, we did keep saying one thing about Kelly. We kept
saying, "He's a good little old watchdog." Heaven
knows why we thought so, except that he barks at the
drop of a soufflé. In fact, when he's in the basement a
stiff toothbrush on the third floor is enough to set him
off into a concerto of deep, murderous growls followed
by loud hysterical yappings. I used to take real pleasure in imagining the chagrin of some poor intruder
who'd bring that cacophony upon himself. Last month
we had an intruder. He got in the porch window and
took twenty-two dollars and my wrist watch while
Kelly, that good little old watchdog, was as silent as a
cathedral. But that's the way it's been.

The first dog I remember well was a large black and
white mutt that was part German shepherd, part English sheep dog, and part collie—the wrong part in
each case. With what strikes me now as unforgivable
whimsey, we called him Ladadog from the title by
Albert Payson Terhune. He was a splendid dog in
many respects but, in the last analysis, I'm afraid he
was a bit of a social climber. He used to pretend that

he was just crazy about us. I mean, if you just left the room to comb your hair he would greet you on your return with passionate lickings, pawings, and convulsive tail-waggings. And a longer separation—let's say you had to go out on the front porch to pick up the mail— would set Ladadog off into such a demonstration of rapture and thanksgiving that we used to worry for his heart.

However, all this mawkish, slobbering sentiment disappeared the moment he stepped over the threshold. I remember we kids used to spot him on our way home from school, chasing around the Parkers' lawn with a cocker friend of his, and we'd rush over to him with happy squeals of "Laddy, oleboy, oleboy, oleboy," and Ladadog would just stand there looking slightly pained and distinctly cool. It wasn't that he cut us dead. He nodded, but it was with the remote air of a celebrity at a cocktail party saying, "Of *course* I remember you, and how's Ed?"

We kept making excuses for him and even worked out an elaborate explanation for his behavior. We decided that Ladadog didn't see very well, that he could only recognize us by smell and that he couldn't smell very well in the open air. However, the day came when my mother met Ladadog in front of the A & P. She was wearing her new brown coat with the beaver collar, and, lo and behold, Ladadog greeted her with joy and rapture. After that we just had to face the truth —that dog was a snob.

He also had other peculiarities. For instance, he saved lettuce. He used to beg for lettuce and then he would store it away in the cellar behind the coalbin. I don't know whether he was saving up to make a salad or what, but every so often we'd have to clean away a small, soggy lump of decayed vegetation.

And every time the phone rang he would run from wherever he was and sit there beside the phone chair, his tail thumping and his ears bristling, until you'd make some sort of an announcement like "It's just the

Let's say you had to go out on the front porch
to pick up the mail . . .

Hoover man'' or ''Eileen, it's for you.'' Then he would immediately disappear. Clearly, this dog had put a call in to someone, but we never did figure out who.

Come to think of it, the dog that gave us the most trouble was a beagle named Murphy. As far as I'm concerned, the first thing he did wrong was to turn into a beagle. I had seen him bouncing around in the excelsior of a pet-shop window, and I went in and asked the man, ''How much is that adorable fox terrier in the window?'' Did he say, ''That adorable fox terrier is a beagle?'' No, he said, ''Ten dollars, lady.'' Now, I don't mean to say one word against beagles. They have rights just like other people. But it is a bit of a shock when you bring home a small ball of fluff in a shoebox, and in three weeks it's as long as the sofa.

Murphy was the first dog I ever trained personally, and I was delighted at the alacrity with which he took to the newspaper. It was sometime later that we discovered, to our horror, that—like so many dogs—he had grasped the letter but not the spirit of the thing. Until the very end of his days he felt a real sense of obligation whenever he saw a newspaper—*any* newspaper—and it didn't matter where it was. I can't bring myself to go into the sordid details, except to mention that we were finally compelled to keep all the papers in the bottom of the icebox.

He had another habit that used to leave us open to a certain amount of criticism from our friends, who were not dogophiles. He never climbed up on beds or chairs or sofas. But he always sat on top of the piano. In the beginning we used to try to pull him off of there. But after a few noisy scuffles in which he knocked a picture off the wall, scratched the piano, and smashed a lamp, we just gave in—only to discover that, left to his own devices, he hopped up and down as delicately as a ballet dancer. We became quite accustomed to it, but at parties at our house it was not unusual to hear a guest remark, ''I don't know what I'm drinking but I think I see a big dog on the piano.''

It's not just our own dogs that bother me. The dogs I meet at parties are even worse. I don't know what I've got that attracts them; it just doesn't bear thought. My husband swears I rub chopped meat on my ankles. But at every party it's the same thing. I am sitting in happy conviviality with a group in front of the fire when all of a sudden the large mutt of mine host appears in the archway. Then, without a single bark of warning, he hurls himself upon me. It always makes me think of that line from *A Streetcar Named Desire*— "Baby, we've had this date right from the beginning." My martini flies into space and my stockings are torn before he finally settles down peacefully in the lap of my new black faille. I blow out such quantities of hair as I haven't swallowed and glance at my host, expecting to be rescued. He murmurs, "Isn't that wonderful? You know, Brucie is usually so distant with strangers."

At a dinner party in Long Island last week, after I had been mugged by a large sheep dog, I announced quite piteously, "Oh dear, he seems to have swallowed one of my earrings." The hostess looked really distressed for a moment, until she examined the remaining earring. Then she said, "Oh I think it will be all right. It's small and it's round."

Nowadays if I go anywhere I just ask if they have a dog. If they do, I say, "Maybe I'd better keep away from him—I have this bad allergy." This does not tend to endear me to my hostess. In fact, she behaves rather as though she'd just discovered that I was listed in "Red Channels." But it is safer. It really is.

6. The Kerr-Hilton

EVER SINCE Gilbert was born we had been looking for a larger house, and we knew what we wanted. I wanted a house that would have four bedrooms for the boys, all of them located some distance from the living room —say in the next county somewhere.

I also yearned for space near the kitchen for a washer, a dishwasher, a freezer, a dryer, and a large couch where I could lie on sunny days and listen to them all vibrate.

Walter, on the other hand, was looking for a place where the eggs would be near the range and the range would be near the telephone so that he could fry his eggs and perhaps even eat them while he answered the thirty-eight phone calls he always gets during breakfast. The calls are never important, but they make up in quantity what they lack in quality. Mostly, it's somebody from one of the broadcasting companies who wants him to appear on a television show at five-thirty in the morning or it's a young man named Eugene Klepman who wants Walter's advice about making a musical based on the first three books of the Old Testament. One way or another he hasn't had breakfast in seven years. This might have had the salutary effect of causing him to lose weight, except that he munches peanut brittle all morning in an effort—he says—to gain enough strength to cope with the people who will call while he's eating lunch.

I don't know that the twins had any very concrete picture of their dream house. One thing they *didn't* want was a playroom, since they really prefer to cut up the new magazines in the middle of the kitchen floor while I'm trying to serve dinner. I have tried to explain to them about playrooms, but I can see that the mere notion of a room in which there was nothing to break fills them with panic and frustration.

Gilbert may have had strong preferences, but at seventeen months he was a boy of few words. In fact, they were so few I can list them. He could say, with ringing clarity: cooky, ice keem, no, kolly-pop, *no*, Cokee-Cola, NO, and take-a-walk. Of course this taciturnity has certain real advantages. It means, for one thing, that he can't sing a single verse of "Davey Crockett." And we're hoping that by the time he's five—which I think of as the age of treason—the whole thing will have blown over.

Christopher, now that he is eight and quite sophisticated, has at one time or another expressed a desire for a house that would have no sinks or bathtubs. But, as I keep telling him, such a sanctuary would be hard to come by these days.

In the beginning we made the usual mistake of looking at houses we could afford. I am working on a proposition, hereafter to be known as Kerr's law, which states in essence: all the houses you can afford to buy are depressing. For months and months we followed happy, burbling real estate agents through a succession of ruins which, as the agents modestly conceded, "needed a little paint and paper to make them happy." These houses invariably had two small dark living rooms and one large turn-of-the-century kitchen—and I don't mean the nineteenth century. At my various feeble protests that I would like to get away from a pump in the kitchen, the agent was usually very stern. "If you want six bedrooms in your price range," he'd say, "you must expect an older house." Well, I did expect an older house, but not any older, say, than the battle at Harper's Ferry. I remember one house in Larchmont. No one knew when it had been built, but it had two cells in the basement and a tunnel going down to the Sound for the protection of runaway slaves. Looking back, it seems to me that we should have snapped up that place. With four boys, you never know when you're going to need an escape hatch.

By this time we had been looking for nearly a year, and I had just about decided to wait until the boys were married and buy a *smaller* place. The one afternoon we had an appointment to go back and see a house in which we had been mildly interested. There was some little mix-up on time and we found ourselves with half an hour to kill. At this point the real estate agent, Mrs. McDermott, suggested, "Look, there's a crazy house down on the water. It's nothing you'd be interested in, but would you like to see it just for the laughs?" We said, "Oh, sure—if it's that funny."

Well, we got our laugh, starting the minute we pulled up at the front door. It was a huge brick castle in which clock towers and cupolas and tilted chimneys all blended in a style that Walter was later to describe as neogingerbread.

The front door itself was a tremendous carved-oak affair that looked like the door of St. Gabriel's Church —not unreasonably, since it turned out that it *was* the door of St. Gabriel's Church. Hanging on the door was a large, hideous lion's head. This seemed to be a knocker, but when Walter went to knock it, it fell off into his arms. (It's since been put back.) Eventually someone on the inside heard our halloos, and the door swung slowly open on its great hinges with a whistle and a creak like that gate on *Inner Sanctum*. We stepped inside. I jumped back suddenly to avoid colliding with two cannon and fell into a gun rack. As we were picking up the guns, we noticed the courtyard.

Though it hadn't been apparent from the outside, the house was actually built on four sides around a large open court. Tudor-ranch, you might call it. Many of the walls bordering on the court were of glass, so that the great outdoors seemed constantly to be coming indoors. Normally, I wouldn't have minded a bit, except that this particular courtyard strongly resembled an M-G-M set for *The Prodigal*. There were Persian idols and towering stone cats and Chinese bells and gargoyles, and I expected Edmund Purdom to step out of the fish pool any minute. The fish pool, by the way, drained into a smaller fish pool through a diving helmet which then lighted up. It took us some time to tear ourselves away from this bit of Old Baghdad, particularly as Walter had got his foot caught in the diving helmet.

Working our way back through a room that had been completely assembled from an old Hudson River steamboat, we saw the living room—or rather, we saw the fireplace, which was all you could see in the living room. It was a monster rising two stories high. At the base there were two large stone arches over which loomed layers and layers of brick, interrupted by occasional layers of fieldstone, and in the center of which reposed a series of Dutch tiles depicting, I am told, Death and the Knight. Hovering over this was more brick in a variety of colors, leading the eye to a vast blue panel, quite near the ceiling, onto which had been glued thirteen ceramic angels. (They may be muses; we've never climbed high enough to see.) Somehow or other, the final effect was so like the grotto at Lourdes that you felt there ought to be crutches hanging on it.

At one moment Walter was leaning against a section of oak paneling in order to get a better view of the ceiling, the ceiling being composed entirely of carved pink and gold plaques representing the Vanderbilt coat of arms (it had come from the old Vanderbilt place in New York City). I called to him to notice the selection of gilt semi-Byzantine pillars, some of which supported the balcony while others were just standing there, only to discover that he had quietly vanished. The section of paneling had swung back into an old secret closet, and so had he.

The next thing we knew we were exploring a winding staircase, at the foot of which gleamed a glass box containing the works of a clock. "Oh, I forgot to tell you about that clock," remarked Mrs. McDermott. "It plays the duet from *Carmen* at noon." ... "Of course," I chirped, "and how about Beethoven's Fifth at six?" As it turned out, though, she was merely stating the facts. The clock was connected electrically to a thirty-two-bell carillon in the courtyard which—what with one thing and another—I hadn't even noticed.

After that, we passed through a number of conventional rooms. That is to say, except for the Venetian paneling and the iron gates and the portholes and the stained-glass windows, they might have looked just like any other rooms.

Not the dining room, though. Even in this house it was something special. It was entirely lined with mirrors, not only the walls and the ceiling but the top of the dining-room table as well. I was sure that if you glanced down while you were eating, you could see your inlays reflected all over the room. Walter was fascinated. He kept trying to calculate the number of possible reflections. Obviously he was imagining an infinity of images like the boy on the Cliquot Club bottle who is carrying a bottle with a boy on the bottle who is carrying a bottle, etc., etc. He'd say, "Now, let's imagine you're here at breakfast in your old pajamas with your hair in curlers—how many times?" It was staggering, all right. And we were staggering as we got back out on the sidewalk.

Mrs. McDermott turned to us and asked playfully, "Well, what did you think of that?" Walter and I replied in the perfect unison of a Greek chorus, "It's the nuttiest house we ever saw, we'll buy it." Where-

You're not serious, you're out of your minds!

upon she, faithless to every real estate code, screamed, "You're not serious, you're out of your minds!" Walter said, "We're out of our minds, but we're serious."

As we drove home in a trance, Walter finally broke the silence by asking fearfully, "What do you suppose we like about it?" But by this time I knew. Somewhere among the bells and the gargoyles I had become aware of the fact that it was just the house for us. For one thing, the master bedroom was completely isolated in a wing by itself. Then there was a room off the garage that would make a wonderful playroom, and another one off the living room that would make a perfect den. Nearly every room in the house had a glorious, sweeping view of the Sound, and the dining room— miracles of miracles—had a heavy oak floor which obviously would never require a rug.

Now one of the problems of my life is trying to keep the dining-room rug clean. A friend of mine solved a similar problem in the living room by buying a rug the color of Coca-Cola. But it's not really possible to find a rug the color of mashed potatoes, Russian dressing and butter-pecan ice cream. (Though this is a project I do wish some enterprising rug company would mull over.)

When we're at home we always eat dinner with the boys. Heaven knows why. It will eventually give us ulcers, and even in my most optimistic moments I can't honestly believe that their childhood is being enriched by the warm and tender memory of those family meals accompanied by a steady stream of directives: "No, you can't make a sandwich with your potato chips"; "Yes, you have to eat the tassels on the broccoli"; "Don't put your finger in the plate—all right, don't put your *thumb* in the plate"; "No, we don't have carrots *all* the time," and so on and on.

In dealing with our children, we don't lean on any of the more advanced methods of child psychology. I tend to remember the immortal words of that philosopher and father, Moss Hart, who once announced that in dealing with *his* children he kept one thing in mind: "We're bigger than they are, and it's *our* house."

I do read in the textbooks that even an occasional spanking tends to make a child feel insecure. This may be so. On the other hand, if a child really needs a whacking and doesn't get it, *I* feel very insecure. Normally, our boys accept discipline with resignation, even detachment. There was a night, though, when the twins had been sent to their room for some infraction (they had removed the caps from a whole case of beer, as I recall) and we could hear revolt brewing. Johnny muttered, "Well, I'm not going to give *her* any more kisses. Col, you tell her you won't give her any more kisses either." And then I heard Col say, in his croaky little voice, "I couldn't do that. It would break her heart."

We didn't consult the twins about the house, but we did take Chris over on one of our subsequent tours of inspection. He wandered over the whole place in utter silence, and even on the way home couldn't be prodded into venturing an opinion. Some hours later a single sentence escaped him:

"Compared to that house, Camelot was mod*ren*."

But then, Chris's avowed goal in life is to become a comedian. I don't know what's happened to the youth of America. I can remember when boys wanted to be policemen or firemen or something respectable. Lately, Chris rattles off everything in a quick, flat patter, obviously trying to approximate the cadences of his idol, Bob Hope. I say to him, "Christopher, don't you dare lie on that new bedspread," and he snaps back with, "I will always tell the truth on this bedspread." I say, "Christopher, you're filthy!" and he remarks, "I resent that. I don't deny it, but I resent it."

Any lingering doubts we may have had about buying the house quickly disappeared when we discovered that nobody really wanted to sell it. It belonged to Charles B. King, a charming old gentleman who had been an inventor and an early associate of Henry Ford (he got out just *before* the nick of time, as I understand it) and who had taken over the property in the early twenties, when it was still the stable and coach house of an estate that has since become the Larchmont Shore Club. King was a collector and world traveler, and he clearly never passed a junk shop or a cathedral without picking up something for his fairy-tale house. He built it up piece by piece, whim by whim. His affairs were now being handled by a committee, and, through negotiations that lasted as long as the San Francisco Conference, we discovered that on Mondays and Wednesdays the committee was willing to sell the house but couldn't agree on a price. The rest of the time the committee was agreed on a price but wouldn't sell.

It seemed as though we were permanently stalemated when a friend of ours called on the phone one morning to say, "You know that house you were trying to buy? Well, it burned down last night."

We were stricken (particularly as we had just sold our own house), and we rushed right over. At first glance it looked as though Nuremberg had been bombed all over again, but we finally realized that only one side of the quadrangle, plus portions of two other sides, had really been destroyed, and that the living quarters proper had barely been touched. Faced with the problem of rebuilding, the committee turned around and agreed to sell us the house, charred timbers and all.

Having made up our minds that we were going to go ahead no matter what anybody said, we began to ask the opinions of our friends and relations. My father, who is a contractor, marched glumly around the house muttering darkly about stresses and strains, so I cheerfully pointed to the water and said, "But, Dad—look at the view you get." He contented himself with observing that during hurricanes we'd get the view right in the basement.

Most of our friends agreed that, like New York, it was a great place to visit but you wouldn't want to live there. "Maybe you could charge a shilling and show people through," one said. Someone else had a really bleak thought. He walked up and down the echoing living room and announced, "Obviously the only people you'll ever be able to entertain here are actors. Nobody else could be heard."

I have a friend who is a decorator, and I was sure he'd be fascinated by the place. I showed him through, and then waited for him to exclaim and extoll. "Well?" I asked brightly. "Well?" He paused with the air of a man being torn between the demands of friendship and of honesty. "I will say this," he at last said, "you have a lot of interesting horizontals."

After that I stopped asking for opinions, but I didn't stop getting them. We began to bring contractors in to get bids on the reconstruction. Without exception, they all burst into peals of hilarity the minute they set foot inside the door. I'd say, "Now, we want to eliminate this door and put in linoleum," and they'd shout, "Holy fright, take a gander at that ceiling." I'd say, "Now, about the linoleum," and they'd say, "My brother-in-law is a junk dealer. Would *he* get a bang out of this!" Some days we never got back to the linoleum at all.

Eventually, we worked out a system. To this day, when somebody comes to the door—a new milkman or a boy from the delivery service—we take the milk or sign for the parcel and then stop everything while we show him right through the house. It's much simpler than having him hover around the kitchen asking questions for twenty minutes.

We knew we were moving on May first, but we hadn't been able to do any packing beforehand because we were working so furiously to finish the first act of our projected musical comedy, *Goldilocks*. (Don't miss it when it opens sometime in 1965.) Working on the musical means that we first of all locate the four children and threaten them with violence and sudden death if they come near us. Then we take coffee and cigarettes and hide in the den. Walter sits at the typewriter in gloom and in silence. I stretch out on a couch and leaf an old copy of the Sears, Roebuck catalogue—in gloom and in silence. Eventually one of us thinks of a line and the other groans and out of this jolly companionship comes reams of material, most of which is rewritten thirty-eight times.

I had planned to take the week off just before the move so that I could pack, and perhaps discover what was in those boxes in the attic marked "Sloms, drinds and blue jeans." On the first of the week, however, I came down with a sodden cold which quickly developed into bronchitis. I piteously begged the doctor for pleurocillin or peneomyacin or one of those things that cost eight dollars for six tablets and cure you overnight. The doctor just shrugged his shoulders and murmured sympathetically, "Now if you only had pneumonia—" Unfortunately, I didn't have pneumonia, so I was sick all week and we had to have the moving men do all the packing. And a conscientious crew they turned out to be. When we arrived at the new house, I discovered that at five dollars a carton they had carefully packed, in excelsior, a fine assortment of broken crayons, three wheels from an old tractor, the back covers of fourteen coloring books, odd slats from an old Venetian blind, and a number of empty tins left over from Birdseye frozen chicken pies.

My mother came to help us move. This was a great boon, except that there is something wrong with her metabolism. She is not able to work for more than nineteen hours without stopping. During this period she is sustained by nothing more than several gallons of hot tea, which she consumes while on the top rungs of ladders or deep inside crates. By midnight, when I was ready to sob with fatigue, it was nothing for Mother to announce cheerfully, "Well, what do you say we clean out the garage?" She was a little disconcerted,

—out of this jolly companionship comes
reams of material . . .

though, when she discovered she wasn't able to pick up a television set, and I heard her moaning softly, "Jean, I'm afraid I'm beginning to slow down." I don't know whether it's true, but we can hope.

On the whole, moving day was like a scene from an old Mack Sennett comedy, with the four men moving our stuff in and the three men moving *their* stuff out plus the contractors and the plumber who was installing the washer and the little boy from next door who came to show us where the bird's nests were and the men from Macy's who brought the wrong beds. Not to mention the engineers who came to fix the furnace and spent an hour and a half looking for it. I had one man bring four loads up to the attic before I discovered that he was there to install the television set.

Walter had a show to review that night, so at six o'clock we just dropped everything and went into New York, leaving Mabel—our combination maid, housekeeper, nurse, companion, and friend—to find the children and find the food and find the beds. She also had to find the fuse box, since only one light was working and that was out in the burned-out section of the garage. She, talented girl, found it too. By the time we returned home at one o'clock in a driving sleet every light in the house was blazing away cheerfully. We were in our new home.

That was some time ago. Since then we've learned quite a few things. We've learned about the master bedroom, for instance. To get to it, you climb a short flight of stairs, then a longer flight of stairs, take a detour through a balcony, and then muster your strength for the last upward pull. To get down, you reverse the process. Nowadays whenever we come down in the morning and discover we've forgotten something, we either do without it or go out and buy a new one.

We've learned what happens to young boys. Everybody warned us that we could expect a lot of broken bones the moment the lads started to clamber over the balcony and out among the gargoyles. As it happened, we weren't in the house a week when Johnny broke his arm. It didn't happen here, though—it happened in nursery school. A four-and-a-half-year-old blonde named Cleo had had her eye on Johnny. On Monday she gave him a penny. On Tuesday she gave him a Davy Crockett button. On Wednesday she pushed him into a box and broke his arm in two places. Clearly this girl means business, and I think Johnny should keep the hell away from her. I asked him recently what ever happened to Cleo and he replied solemnly, "I don't know, but I hear she's going to have to sit in a corner for the rest of her life." And good enough for her, too.

Other things have happened. Two dogwood trees and one lilac bush that we didn't even know were there have bloomed and faded. The squirrels in the bell tower have had more squirrels. Sometimes I think the carpenters have had more carpenters. There were three or four to start with and today there are six.

But the roof is finally on, the garage has been restored, and most of the charred timber has been carted away—much to the dismay of the children, who used to make forts with it and emerge after ten minutes looking like Welsh coal miners. Oh, things are progressing. Even Gilbert notices it. This morning he pointed at the peacocks on the new wallpaper in the breakfast room and murmured, "Nice doggies, nice doggies."

Of course the playroom isn't finished and the den isn't even begun and all the bricking and painting remain to be done. By my own private calculations (I multiply the number of carpenters by the number of days in a week and divide by the cost of one panel of wallboard) I figure that the workmen will be here for seven years, give or take a few quarantines. On the one hand, I do get just a shade weary of seeing old tarpaulins over all the floors all the time, not to mention little piles of sand in the pantry and big piles of lumber under the piano. On the other hand, when I consider what gentle, personable people carpenters are, and what splendid companions they will be for the children as they are growing up, I begin to see a plan and a purpose in it all.

7. The care and feeding of producers

I DON'T THINK there's been a single book written in the last five days on how to write a play or how not to write a play. To me this is symptomatic. Word is getting around and soon we'll all have to face the fact: everybody *knows* how to write a play. At least, everybody *I* know is writing a play, including several people who have families to support. Our milkman, for instance, is writing a play about the time that he and his wife and his mother-in-law were snowed in for the whole winter in a small cabin on the upper Delaware. Nobody came in, nobody went out, and they lived on dry fruitcake and melted snow. Oh, what a year that was! The author himself put it rather neatly when he said, "We had a million laughs."

But, in the face of such universal application, why are there so few successful playwrights? Well, for one thing, there are dozen of books which explain to the uninitiated the value of characterization, the importance of climax, the necessity for double-spacing the script—but where is a young playwright going to learn the really basic things, the important things, like how to have lunch with a producer?

At first glance, it should seem that lunching with a producer should be a simple enough business. Actual-

The care and feeding of producers

ly, it is a delicate ritual, as deliberate and formalized in its ways as a pavane.

To begin with, the unproduced playwright should always order a drink. The producer will expect to have one and it irritates him to drink alone. Having ordered the drink, however, you must be careful not to touch it. Otherwise, he will assume that you are an alcoholic, and while he bears no grudge against alcoholics personally—some of his best friends are alcoholics—he nevertheless has poignant memories of that author who disappeared into Kaysey's bar at ten after eleven on opening night in New Haven and never was heard of more.

Somewhere between the appetizer and the main course, the producer will endeavor to put you at your ease by making general conversation about the current season, with special reference to the biggest hits. Here is where you should be on your guard. If he wishes to reveal his rare magnanimity of spirit by saying a few kind words about *My Fair Lady, let* him—but on no account agree with him. Remember that no matter what he says (and what he says is, ''Hits are good for the theatre, we can't have too many hits'') he still regards any success not his as an affront to him personally, an attack on everything he stands for, a scourge, a plague, and very possibly Communist-inspired.

It's not that he doesn't grasp that, in the logic of things, other managers will have a hit from time to time; in his frame of reference, this is a prospect as inevitable as death and taxes, and just about as appetizing. The rule, then, is if you can't say anything bad about a current hit, say nothing at all. This helpful principle also applies to a variety of other subjects, including drama critics, stagehands, Joshua Logan, child actors, eight-o'clock curtains, and *Variety's* practice of printing weekly box-office reports.

If you wish to inch your way into his regard, you might say, ''I know people rave about *My Fair Lady,* but personally I got more kick out of that arena production of *Alcestis* done with masks in the original Greek.'' Everybody else within earshot will think you're gone off your rocker, but the producer will recognize instantly that you are an independent spirit worth cultivating.

Now, as a mark of his growing confidence in you, he may be willing to explain why his last show got bad notices. If he seems in any way reluctant to launch into this topic closest to his heart, prod him a little. If necessary, take your finger out of that dike and ask him point-blank, ''Mr. Spellbound, I saw your production of *Peanut Butter and Crackers*. The audience *adored* it. Why do you suppose the Boys were so tough on it?'' This should provide you with at least an hour of uninterrupted listening pleasure.

To the secular mind, it seems clear enough that a play gets bad notices for any one of the three reasons: (1) the script was bad; (2) the production was bad; (3) the critics are idiots. The producer has a different theory altogether. He grants, heaven knows, that there isn't a critic alive with an I.Q. higher than 78, but nevertheless he doesn't blame the reviewers. He blames all his troubles, past and present, on ''that opening-night audience.''

He feels that his show, which looked like a million dollars on Saturday night in Philadelphia, turned up on Forty-fourth Street looking like change for a nickel because ''half of those people had seen the show *three* times, for Heaven's sake, and knew all the jokes, and the rest of those zombies haven't laughed publicly since 1938, and how the hell can an actor give a good performance under those conditions?'' If you should happen to detect the one tiny flaw in this theory (that precisely the same chic, enameled people, give or take a couple of actors' agents, were in attendance on the opening night of *Separate Tables* or *Auntie Mame*), just keep it locked in your heart.

Eventually, or a minute or two before your nerves give out, the conversation will get around to *your* play.

At this point, the producer will adopt an intimate, even cuddly tone. "Dear boy," he will say, "do you know why I like this play?" (Many producers address all playwrights as "dear boy," a practice which is disconcerting only if you happen to be a girl.) You probably won't be able to resist asking, "No, why?" but he warned that the answer may scare you. If you have written what you think of as a light comedy, he is apt to tell you, "Because, dear boy, it has honest guts, plenty of raw meat—it hit me right *here*" (indicating an area somewhere south of the pancreas). On the other hand, if it's a melodrama, he will unnerve you by remarking, "I figure it this way, if it makes *me* laugh, it'll make everybody laugh."

With this, and almost before you can say *Long Day's Journey into Night*, you will be deep into the always touchy subject of revisions. Keep in mind—in all justice to the producer—that's he's not necessarily being picky if he wants the script reworked. There are very few plays that couldn't be improved by some cuts and changes. Therefore, if he says, "Look, the first act is impossible, the second act is poor, but the scene at the end of the third act is swell," that's reasonable. You agree on *something*. But suppose the dialogue goes like this:

HIM: You've got a great story here, but I hate those Civil War costumes. Why does it have to be in 1860?

YOU: Because it's about Mary Todd Lincoln.

HIM: Very well—if you don't *want* criticism. Listen, you've got a great story here, but the characters are ridiculous and I tell you frankly—those Civil War costumes are death at the box office.

YOU: But you can't separate the story from the character of Mary Lincoln. This is based on actual fact and——

HIM: Dear boy, let me tell you something. If a story has universality, it can be set in any period. How about 1901?

YOU: What happened then?

—I figure it this way, if it makes *me* laugh, it'll make
everybody laugh.

HIM: McKinley was shot. And his wife was a hell of an interesting character.

In this circumstance it is probably prudent to assume that you two aren't meant for each other.

Since it is evident that not all producers possess the necessary amount of shrewdness, technical know-how, and locked-in goodness, how do you know when you've got the right one? There are producers who can get a two-year run out of what was formerly a television script. There are producers who can open a musical in June without an advance, without stars, without theatre parties, and without Cole Porter—and two days later scalpers will be getting $50 for a pair of seats next January. Then, of course, there is the producer who will have to close a show out of town that employs the combined talents of Ethel Merman, Mary Martin, and Menasha Skulnik.

How do you recognize the richer, milder, longer-lasting type?

First of all, a producer shouldn't be too young or too old. If, in discussing the script, your producer-to-be announces reverently, "This part would be perfect for Maude," he's too old. If, lamentably, you are already contractually tied to this Voice of the Past, be careful not to make any flat statements of fact—like, "You don't mean Maude Adams, good heavens, she's *dead!*" The best procedure is to lead him upward and onward to 1958 by a process of gentle questioning like "Do you mean, sir, the Maude Adams of *The Little Minister* or the Maude Adams of *Peter Pan?*"

Of course, a really advanced case will never come farther than November 1925, when Grace George was so delicious in *She Had to Know*. A playwright of my acquaintance made the mistake of suggesting to his man that they hire Shelley Winters for his new melodrama and was rather disconcerted when the producer asked politely, "What *are* shelley winters?"

Then again, a producer can be too young. I myself had a producer, a charming redhead, who was so young that she contracted mumps from one of the child actors and missed the out-of-town opening.

Any male producer under thirty-five is probably a genius and should be avoided like a traffic summons. Your true "genius" was frightened at an early age by Moss Hart and has subsequently nursed a deep distrust for the commercial theatre. (By the commercial theatre we mean anything that is successful and pays off.) He is full of random schemes for taking the best of André Gide and turning it into a musical. He is also fiercely dedicated to the proposition that Shakespeare could be sold to the tired businessman if only it were imaginatively produced—"Jackie Gleason, *there's* your King Lear!" In fact, come to think of it, if he likes your play there must be something the matter with it.

Speaking for myself, I am wary of producers who come in pairs. (And any number greater than two is absolutely unthinkable; in this case you have a pride of producers, like a pride of lions, with roughly the same inherent hazards.) It is extremely difficult to keep your bearings when you are dealing with two men. You've been informed that one of them is lovable and the other one is very tough (but shrewd).

The difficulties begin when you try to figure out which is which. Just when you think you *know,* the lovable one informs you that Abe Burrows has been reworking your dialogue and will have to be listed as co-author and the shrewd one tells you his favorite evening in the theatre was spent at "Shangri-La."

And what if you get the perfect producer, a gentleman of consummate artistry and matchless taste who is, in addition, loyal, helpful, courteous, brave, clean, and reverent? He buys your script. He persuades Charles Boyer and Rosalind Russell to play the leads. He hires Jo Mielziner to design the sets and Elia Kazan to direct. He then has a big, whopping flop. There you are, all alone on the grim morning after, with no handy alibis, forced to face the cold, implacable truth—that little play of yours was a dog.

8. One half of two on the aisle

IN MY SHORT and merry life in the theatre, I have discovered that there are two sharply contrasting opinions about the place of the drama critic. While in some quarters it is felt that the critic is just a necessary evil, most serious-minded, decent, talented theatre people agreed that the critic is an unnecessary evil. However, if there is some room for argument about the value of the critic, there is none whatever about the value of the critic's wife. To the producer, in particular, it is painful enough that the reviewer must bring his own glum presence to the theatre, but the thought that he will also bring his wife and that she, too, will occupy a free seat is enough to cool the cockles of his heart and send him back on a soft diet. "What if a doctor had to bring his wife along when he performed an operation?" he will ask you. "Can't you see her sitting there murmuring, 'Here's a nice suture, dear, and why don't you try this clamp?'"

In their innermost souls, the producer and the press agents are convinced that the wife has a bad effect on the critic and consequently a bad effect on the notice. Of course, not all critics have wives; some of them habitually attend the theatre in the company of pretty actresses, a practice which is thought to be not only suitable but even, on occasion, inspiring.

It isn't that anyone believes a wife's influence is direct or intentional. Presumably no one has suggested that it is her practice to tuck her spouse into a cab at eleven o'clock with the stern admonition, "Now you hurry right back to that little office and say what a bad play this was, hear?" No, the whole thing is much more intangible than that, and I'm afraid it boils down to the sobering fact that the producer feels that the mere physical presence of a wife depresses the critic, lowers his spirits, clogs his areas of good will, and leaves his head rattling with phrases like "witless," "tasteless," and "below the level of the professional theatre."

On the other hand, just let some wife absent herself from the happy revelers at an opening and you will see consternation settle like a fine dew upon producer and press agent alike. Souls are searched. Old wounds are probed. Is the jig up? Have runners been coming in from Philadelphia with the bad word? Have those preview audiences been squealing? Clearly somebody talked. The lady has had fair warning and is at home with a good book.

It is my impression that my own attendance record is rather higher than the average. This can be explained by the fact that I have those four small children and naturally have to get out a lot. When my husband first went on a newspaper, and for several years thereafter, I brought my lark-like disposition and gooey good will to every single solitary show that opened. Lately, however, I've begun to develop a small, cowardly instinct for self-preservation, and I find that there are two kinds of plays I can bear not to see: plays about troubled adolescents who can't find themselves, and plays about the Merchant of Venice.

During this past summer we paid a visit to Stratford, England, and saw a number of plays not including

—I brought my lark-like disposition and gooey good will to
every single solitary show that opened.

The Merchant of Venice. It seemed to make the whole
trip worth while. I have friends, old-time theatregoers
who have seen every Hamlet since Forbes-Robertson,
and they love to sit around and reminisce about the way
Leslie Howard played the ghost scene and how Gielgud
read the speech to the players. Now, I hope to spend my
twilight years reminiscing about the Shylocks I haven't
seen. Donald Wolfit, Luther Adler, Clarence Derwent—
oh, it's a splendid gallery already and I expect to add
to it before I'm through.

As everyone knows, one of the chief problems of going
to the theatre with a critic is getting out of there a
split second after the curtain comes down or, if the
show is a very long one, a split second before. Lately I've
become very adept at judging the precise line of dialogue on which to start pulling the sleeves of my coat
out from under the lady next to me. This might be
when an actress says, "In future years, when you
speak of me, be kind," or when an actor says, "Now
that I've got you, darling, I'll never let you go," although I have known shows in which he let her go for
another ten minutes after that.

Then follows a wild scramble down a dark and
crowded aisle. I used to forge stolidly ahead, having
developed a technique for this sort of thing in Ohrbach's
basement, but one night, when I felt I had Walter firmly by the hand and was propelling him out into the
traffic, I heard a plaintive voice muttering, "Hey, lady,
gee, lady, please!" I looked up to discover that I had
Farley Granger firmly by the hand. It's things like that
that make one pause and reconsider.

After the show, most wives go out with their friends
or go home to their peaceful apartments. I tag along to
the office because we live in Larchmont and neither
one of us wants to make the trip back alone. Obviously,
if I were planning to influence my husband, my golden
opportunity would come during the cab ride over to the

office. The only trouble is that he immediately assumes the yogi-like silence and the glazed manner of a sandhog in a decompression chamber.

I used to think he was going into shock, but I have gradually gleaned that he is just trying to think of an opening sentence. I wouldn't dream of breaking the cathedral hush that surrounds us. However, if there is one thing a cab driver does not seem to recognize, it is a cathedral hush. All the cab drivers we get at ten forty-five in the evening are sports, bon vivants, and raconteurs. One man the other night had a really tantalizing story about how he had to drive a burro to Riverdale. My only question is, where are all those gay blades during the six-o'clock rush hour in front of the Biltmore?

Once my husband is at his desk, he sets to work immediately, furiously consulting the dozens of penciled notes he makes during the show on intricately folded yellow paper. I glanced at the notes one evening and the first one said, "Why he shedelepp so often, especially in the speckeldiff?" I only hope he doesn't lose them some night. They might be found, and how would he prove they're not atomic secrets?

Anyway, while he's working, I'm not idle. I sit at an empty desk and read back copies of *The Hollywood Reporter* and draw horses. Sometimes I chat with bright young copyboys, who, it would appear, are serious students of the theatre. The only difficulty is that they want to discuss Toller and Strindberg, whereas, at that hour of the morning, I want to discuss Lindsay and Crouse. Occasionally someone wants to know why Kafka's *The Trial* is never done. Of course I have no figures here, but I have this feeling that it is done all the time. Maybe not.

Then, too, my husband sometimes consults me while he's writing a review. A hoarse shout will come over the partition, "Hey, how do you spell desiccate?" But this is patently ridiculous. If I could spell desiccate I would long since have assumed my rightful place in the world of letters.

An interesting aspect of dramatic criticism is that an actor can remember his briefest notice well into senescence and long after he has forgotten his phone number and where he lives. Thus it is quite a common occurrence for a critic to meet a nice young thing at a party and have her say, "Oh, don't you remember me? You saw me in *The Squared Circle* four years ago and you said I was 'earnest, effortful, and inane.'" Well, that's what makes cocktail parties so interesting.

On the other hand, most people who read more than one drama critic quickly forget who said what. We had an interesting demonstration of this last summer when we met a film actress who was chatting wisely and wittily about the theatre until she reached the subject of a certain musical comedy. Then she declared with some heat, "I don't know what gets into Brooks Atkinson sometimes. Do you know what he said about that show?"

Whereupon she proceeded to recite from memory two paragraphs, word for word, semicolon for semicolon, of Walter's review. After the brief hush that followed this recital, I murmured, "Did Brooks really say that? Well, there you are—even Homer nods," the while my husband made little clicking sounds indicating that he was too shocked even to comment.

In common with the wives of other critics, I am so anxious to indicate that I in no way influence or attempt to influence my husband's opinions that I rather overstate the case and perhaps give the impression that we never discuss the theatre at all—that our conversation is exclusively concerned with stories about our adorable children and the cute way they spilled Three-in-One oil all over the living-room rug, interspersed occasionally with highlights from the world of sport.

The fact is that we have many an intelligent discus-

—you said I was earnest, effortful, and inane.

sion of the play coming home on the train, at which time I have a carbon copy of the review to read. A typical opening gambit in such a conversation would be: "Boy! If *that* was a haunting, luminous performance . . . !"

9. Don Brown's body

AFTER one of those evenings in the theater, an evening that happened to be devoted to a staged reading of Stephen Vincent Benét's *John Brown's Body,* I worked out my own little entertainment:

The curtain—if there is one—rises on a vast blue sky, relieved only by a chaste white balustrade in the foreground. A chorus of pretty girls and pretty boys is seated on folding chairs at one side. Before them, and menacingly near us, stand four lecterns on which scripts that no one will ever look at have been placed. The readers enter, with a dignity that will be theirs to the very end. The first reader begins, however, with a shy, boyish smile.

FIRST READER

In recent years there has been a marked revival of interest in the art of dramatic reading. We have dipped into the treasures of Charles Dickens, George Bernard Shaw, and Stephen Vincent Benét, among others. Yet there is an entire facet of our culture that has never been tapped. I am speaking now of that special genre known as detective fiction, where, as some authorities have pointed out, the interest has lately shifted from "who done it" to "wit what."

There has also been an increasing emphasis on violence and—the woman across the hall has an awfully good word for it—

He glances at a note in his hand

—sex.

As every schoolboy knows, many of these works were written not to be read, but to be inhaled. With this in mind, we offer you *Don Brown's Body*—by Mickey Spillane.

WOMAN READER

Mike Hammer's tune.

FIRST READER

I'm Mike Hammer. I don't take slop from nobody. Like this guy. He ankles up to me on the street. He opens his big ugly yap, and says——

THIRD READER

Pardon me. Have you the correct time?

MIKE

So I kicked him in the mouth and his teeth dropped all over the sidewalk like marbles. Like I say—I don't take slop from nobody.

THIRD READER

Sally Dupre's tune.

WOMAN READER

I know I'm just a broad, Mike. I'm a round-heeled babe with a dirty record. My type comes two thousand dollars a dozen. But I'm clean inside, Mike.

MIKE

I picked her up in Jimmy's bar. She was lying there, so I picked her up. She was in pretty bad shape.

The woman across the hall has an awfully good word for it.

CHORUS

Chanting in unison

Sally Dupre, Sally Dupre,
Her eyes were neither black nor gray,
They were black and blue.

MIKE

I was on a case. When I'm on a case nobody or
nothin' takes my mind off it for a minute.

We went up to her place.

She lived on the St. Regis roof. Sooner or later
some wise guy of a cop is gonna find her up there
and make her come down. But tonight was ours. She
opened her good eye. There was no mistaking that invitation. Her lips were like fresh ketchup on a white
tablecloth. My heart was throbbing like a stubbed toe.

She was waiting for me, a hungry thing. Now there
was nothing between us but us. I spoke:

"You were a member of the Carney gang at the
time that One-Finger Matthews put the finger on
Soft-Spot Sullivan, who was at that time going under
the name of Samuel X. Sullivan and who knifed
Maurie Magnusson in the back of the Easy-Way Garage. The *Queen Mary* docked at eleven forty-six
on the twenty-third, and Joey Jacobson was found in
an abandoned milk truck two years later. What do
you know about Don Brown?"

Her eyes found mine. Down below, the great idiot
city went its old familiar way: birth and death, love
and lust, Martin and Lewis. A long time afterwards
she spoke:

WOMAN READER

Don *Who* Brown?

MIKE

That took me back. The first time I saw Don Brown

was in the locker room at the "Y." He was in my locker.

CHORUS

Not in the good green fields, Don Brown.
Not in the loamy earth, Don Brown,
Under the spike-eared corn—
But in a locker, a long green locker, a lonely long green locker
At the "Y."

MIKE

He'd been dead about three weeks then, judging from the condition of my tennis racket. I reached for a butt.
I was pretty cut up.

CHORUS

Ah, yes, Mike Hammer—ah, yes.
But you were not cut up as Don Brown was cut up.

MIKE

Who'd be next, I wondered? I looked in the next locker. Bill Brown was in that one. One thing was clear. Somebody was going to have to clean out those lockers.
I went out to the street.

CHORUS

Tramp . . . tramp . . . tramp . . .

MIKE

I passed this kid sucking a lollipop. Don Brown dead, and him sucking a lollipop. I rammed it down his throat. I hate injustice.
I walked for hours.

CHORUS

Don Brown's body lies a molderin' at the "Y"——

WOMAN READER
   Don Brown's song.

THIRD READER
   Wish you were here, wish you were here, wish . . .

MIKE
   I went back to the place I call home.

CHORUS
   Tramp . . . tramp . . tramp

MIKE
   The Hairy Arms, Apartment 3-D. I put the key in the
   lock. I opened the door. A gun smashed into my skull.
   Heavy boots ground into my spine. A pair of fists
   tore into my throat.
   I saw something coming toward me. It was a fly
   swatter. This was no ordinary killer.
   I knew then they were after me. And I knew one
   other thing, as they threw me over the third-floor
   railing: they were afraid of me.
   I hit the second-floor landing.
   I hit the first-floor landing.
   I hit the cigar counter.
   The girl behind the cigar counter looked up. There
   was no mistaking that invitation. She was naked beneath that reversible. She reversed the reversible. She
   was still naked. A long time later she spoke:

WOMAN READER
   Bring me your tired, your poor, your huddled
   masses . . .

MIKE
   I went to the office.

CHORUS
   Tramp . . . tramp . . . tramp . . .

MIKE

My secretary, Josephine, was there. She looked up at me.

She was made for me. I tried to be good to Josephine. I used to let her kiss my fingertips every once in a while. But now I carefully put my fingers in my pockets. Josephine would have to wait. There was only one thing on my mind these days.

"What's new on the Don Brown case?"

JOSEPHINE

I checked this morning. He's still there.

CHORUS

Nothing is changed, Don Brown. Nothing is changed. But men are beginning to notice.

In the locker room at the "Y," they're beginning to notice.

It will grow stronger, Don Brown!

MIKE

We went outside.

CHORUS

Tramp . . . tramp . . . tramp . . .

MIKE

My heap was parked at the curb. I had a strong feeling it was wired. I asked Josephine to get in first. She put her foot on the starter.

Boy!

CHORUS

Come Josephine in my flying machine
As *up* we go, *up* we go . . .

MIKE

A long time afterward, she came down. I didn't wait I knew Josephine. She'd pull herself together.

The patrol wagon went by. I thought of Sally. I called her up.

"Sally?"

WOMAN READER
"Mike?"

MIKE
"I'm sweatin' for you, Sally."

WOMAN READER
"I'm clean inside, Mike."

Both hang up.

MIKE
We could talk forever and never get it all said. I was still in the booth when the phone rang. On a hunch, I answered it. It was the killer. He laughed at me. That was all. Laughed at me.

I was no longer a man, I was an ugly thing. I wanted to get his skull between my hands and crack it like a cantaloupe. I wanted to scramble that face like a plate of eggs. I wanted to work him over till his blood ran the color of coffee. That's when it came to me: I hadn't had any breakfast.

I was going into Longchamp's when this tomato waltzes by. She was a tomato surprise. A round white face with yellow hair poured over it like chicken gravy on mashed potatoes. Her racoon coat was tight in all the right places.

I watched her as she disappeared into a doorway. She shut the door. There was no mistaking that invitation.

I followed her in. Inside it was inky darkness. I groped my way across the room. Her lips were warm. Her nose was warm. She barked.

I spoke.

"Down, dammit, down!"

I went back to my place, good old 3-D. I no sooner opened the door than they were at me again. This time I was ready. I smashed my eye into his fist, I forced my ribs into his boot, and the first thing he knew I was flat on my back in the hall. He was standing above me now. He spoke.

THIRD READER

Look, buddy. You do this every night. This is *not* your apartment. You're in 3-D. This is 3-A.

MIKE

After that, everything was like a nightmare. I was sitting in this bar with Sally.
"What'll you have?"

WOMAN READER

"Straight Clorox." I'm clean inside, Mike.

MIKE

Then I was in this strange room with this strange blonde. How did I get here? What kind of a girl was she?

CHORUS

Tramp . . . tramp . . . tramp . . .

MIKE

Then I was in another strange room with another strange blonde. She had just stepped from the tub. There she was as God made her, a mess.
Our eyes were riveted together. I took a step towards her. Then I took another. I fell over the coffee table.
The next thing I knew they had me surrounded. Blondes, brunettes, redheads . . .

THIRD READER

There was no mistaking that invitation.

Her racoon coat was tight in all the right places.

WOMAN READER
Mike Hammer was a man in a million.
Mike Hammer had the strength of ten.
Mike Hammer spoke.

MIKE
No, girls—*no!*

CHORUS

Astonished and exultant

"Glory, glory, hallelujah! . . ."

With a swell in the music, the lights fade.

10. Toujours tristesse

AFTER READING *A Certain Smile* by Francoise Sagan:

I was waiting for Banal. I was feeling rather bored. It was a summer day like any other, except for the hail. I crossed the street.

Suddenly I was wildly happy. I had an overwhelming intuition that one day I would be dead. These large eyes, this bony child's body would be consigned to the sweet earth. Everything spoke of it: the lonely cooing of a solitary pigeon overhead, the stately *bong bong bong* of the cathedral chimes, the loud horn of the motorbus that grazed my thigh.

I slipped into the café, but Banal was late. I was pleased to notice that that simple fact annoyed me.

Banal and I were classmates. Our eyes had met, our bodies had met, and then someone introduced us. Now he was my property, and I knew every inch of that brown body the way you know your own driveway.

A stranger across the booth spoke.

"Monique, what are you staring at, silly girl?"

It was Banal. Curious that I hadn't recognized him. Suddenly I knew why. A revolting look of cheerfulness had twisted and distorted those clear young features until he seemed actually to be smiling.

I couldn't look. I turned my head, but his voice followed me, humbly and at a distance like a spaniel.

"Monique, why did you skip class? We were studying the *Critique of Pure Reason*. It was interesting, but I think Kant offers a false dichotomy. The only viable solution is to provide a synthesis in which experience is impregnated with rationality and reason is ordained to empirical data."

How like Banal to say the obvious. Sometimes as I sat and listened to Banal and his companions trade flippancies, I could feel the boredom grow and swell within me almost as if I had swallowed a beach ball.

Why must we chatter fruitlessly and endlessly about philosophy and politics? I confess that I am only interested in questions that touch the heart of another human being—"Who are you sleeping with?"; "What do you take for quick relief from acid indigestion?"

Banal's voice droned on like a chorus of cicadas on a hot day until finally there was a statement I couldn't ignore.

"Monique, I want you to meet my grandfather, Anatole. My rich grandfather."

A slight, stooped man came toward me. He was no longer middle-aged, but I liked that. I was so tired of these eager boys of fifty. His hair, which was greenish white, might have been unpleasant had there been more of it. As he smiled gently, showing his small, even, ecru teeth, I thought, 'Ah, he's the type that's mad for little girls.' In fact, hadn't I read that he'd had some trouble with the police?

But now, as his dull eyes looked directly into mine and I noticed him idly striking a match on the tablecloth, I realized with a sudden stab of joy that finally I had met a man who was as bored as I was.

And yet, I reminded myself firmly as my heart slid back to earth, this won't last. It can't last. He won't *always* be this bored.

Now Banal was speaking, in his infantile way.

"Do you know Monique has never seen the sea?"

Then a woman spoke, Anatole's wife. She was sitting beside him but I hadn't noticed her because she was

—finally I had met a man who was as bored as I was.

wearing a brown dress and blended into the back of the booth. Her voice was warm, like a caress.

"Why, that's awful that this poor child has never seen the sea. Anatole, darling, you must take her to our little château by the ocean. I won't be able to come because I'm redecorating the town house. But there is plenty of food in the frigidaire, and Monique will be able to see the ocean from the bedroom. Here are the keys."

I liked her for that.

Then they were leaving. Dorette, for that was Anatole's wife's name, had forgotten her gloves, and I admit I felt a pang of jealousy as I noticed the intimate way that Anatole threw them to her.

Now Banal and I were alone. As I suspected, Banal was stormy and full of suspicion. How I hated him when he got this way. He kept asking me, again and again: "Are you sure, Monique, are you really sure that you have never seen the sea?"

But when I assured him, what was the truth, that I never had, he seemed comforted and became once more the sunny, smiling, handsome young man I found so repellent.

We were in Anatole's open car. Overhead the sky was blue as a bruise.

The gleaming white road slipping under our wheels seemed like a ribbon of cotton candy. As I realized we were nearing the château, my heart turned over once quickly and neatly, like a pancake on a griddle.

Anatole's voice seemed to come from a great distance.

"Bored, darling?"

I turned to him.

"Of course—and you?"

His answering smile told me that he was.

And now we were running up the long flight of steps to the château hand in hand like two happy children, stopping only when Anatole had to recover his wind.

At the doorway he paused and gathered me into his

arms. His voice, when he spoke, was like a melody played sweetly and in tune.

"My darling," he said, "I hope I have made it perfectly clear that so far as I am concerned you are just another pickup."

"Of course," I whispered. How adult he was, and how indescribably dear.

So the golden days passed. Mostly we were silent, but occasionally we sat in the twilight and spoke wistfully of Dorette and Banal and what suckers they were.

And who could describe those nights? Never in my relationship with Banal had I felt anything like this. Ah, how rewarding it is to share the bed of a really mature man. For one thing, there was the clatter and the excitement four times a night as he leaped to the floor and stamped on his feet in an effort to get the circulation going. My little pet name for him, now, was Thumper.

The last day dawned cold and bright as a star. Anatole was waiting for me out in the car, so I packed my few belongings, ran a nail file through my curls, and joined him.

What shall I say of the pain of that ride back to Paris? In one sense, we were, both of us, precisely as weary as ever. Yet for the first time it wasn't a shared weariness.

We pulled up to my front door, and then the blow fell.

"Monique," he said, "little one. I *have* been bored with you. Nobody can take that away from us. But the truth is, and I know how this will hurt you, I am even more bored with my wife. I'm going back to her."

He was gone. I was alone. Alone, alone, alone. I was a woman who had loved a man. It was a simple story, prosaic even. And yet somehow I knew I could get a novel out of it.

11. Snowflaketime

I'VE BEEN HEARING that overproduction and high costs are killing the theatre, but I don't know that I actually worried about such things until I saw *Snowflaketime,* the third-grade Christmas play at a school in Larchmont. Then it all came clear to me.

Here was a dazzling production with a chorus of sixty angels in pink gauze, who sang "The First Noel" three times. There was, in addition, a chorus of sixty angels in white gauze, who handed tinsel stars to the angels in pink gauze. There were twenty toy soldiers in red felt uniforms with gold rifles, of whom nineteen were able to march backward. There were 120 dancers "from every land" but mostly from the Balkan countries. There were two scarecrows who had taken tap-dancing and twelve jack-in-the-boxes.

Oh, the whole thing was a "triumph," a "visual delight," and a "stunning success." But of course it will never pay off. Even with a 35-cent top and a capacity house (the house seats 600, with each mother seating one or two extra depending on the width of the mother), they're going to have trouble getting their money back.

Our eight-year-old, who was wrapped in tissue paper and red ribbons and was supposed to be a present, was very distressed because two of the toy soldiers waved at the audience. As my husband remarked, that's the

Full many a moon have I watched on yon hill, and ne'er saw
I such a star as this.

kind of thing they could have cleaned up if they had taken the show to New Rochelle for a couple of weeks. But I imagine they were afraid of those out-of-town losses.

When I was in third grade we didn't gear our productions to the tired business boy. We eschewed extravaganzas. Well, it wasn't so much that we eschewed them; we'd never heard of them. We did the "great" plays—*Nahaliel, the Shepherd, The Shepherd's Gift,* and *The Young Shepherd Boy.* We did them on a shoestring, but with the sense of doom and dedication of some movie actors doing a revival of Ibsen.

I always played the tallest shepherd. I wore my father's old dressing gown and I said, "Full many a moon have I watched on yon hill, and ne'er saw I such a star as this." In an effort to suggest great age, I used to make my voice creak and crackle like a shortwave receiver. All the shepherds were very, very old (the mystery is how they were ever able to watch any sheep) except for one shepherd boy whose characterization changed from year to year.

Sometimes he brought his flute, his only possession, and laid it in the manger. Other years he was lame and brought his crutch. He never came empty-handed and he always had a big scene in which he sobbed and said, "I, Nahaliel, have naught, naught save only this flute [or crook or crutch or whatever it was that year], but freely do I give it to THEE." Then he threw himself down in the straw.

There was a part for an actress. I finally did play Nahaliel, but I started at the bottom. Actually, the first thing I played was part of the scenery. No one was allowed to nail anything to our stage floor, so all the scenery had to be held up by the students. On this occasion I stood behind a large balsam tree and with my free hand shook Lux flakes on Mary and Joseph as they passed, the while making low humming sounds to indicate the inclement state of the weather. My family regarded this triple accomplishment with mixed emotions.

As a matter of fact, I don't think my father's were too mixed. I recall his inquiring bleakly, as the evening of my debut approached, "My God, do you mean we're going to have to get dressed and go all the way up there to see her stand behind a tree?"

Our audiences, generally, came prepared for a profound emotional experience, which may explain why certain locations, directly behind pillars, were in great demand. We always had standees at the rear of the house, even when the auditorium was half empty. But we were proud, and the overhead was low.

Nowadays you hardly see a shepherd at all. As far as the school in Larchmont is concerned, I sensed a shift away from the serious theatre even before Christmas. Some weeks ago our oldest boy came home with the information that he was appearing in a Safety Play. His costume was to be very simple. He was playing a back tire. I asked him what his part consisted of, and he said, "Oh, mostly I just blow out." What I want to know is, will this equip him to play the great parts like Lear or even a front tire? At that, I can scarcely wait for him to play Lear. It'll be so much easier to make the costume.

I suppose that, for the untalented, all costumes are hard. John (age four) came home recently with a yellow slip pinned to his sleeve announcing that his nursery school was going to present *Frosty, the Snowman,* and John was playing—oh, the wonder of it! and why wasn't there a phone call from Sam Zolotow?— *Frosty.*

"You can make the costume out of a worn sheet and an old top hat from the attic," wrote his teacher. The note concluded with the inexplicable statement: "In the first scene Frosty is supposed to be half melted." (Why tell me? As I explained to Johnny, it's the actor's job to characterize. I just make costumes.)

Johnny plowed upstairs ahead of me to find an old

sheet in the linen closet, and the next thing I heard was a sob of anguish. "Mommy"—it was the cry of Oedipus on the heights of Colonus—"our sheets are GREEN!" And so they were. In a burst of whimsey some years ago I had purchased all colored sheets. When I think of those Pepperell people, so full of loud talk about the myriad wonders that can be wrought with colored sheets! I'd like to see them try to make a snowman costume sometime.

But never mind the sheet. What old top hat? What attic? We don't keep old top hats in our attic. We keep academic gowns, white Palm Beach suits that are bound to come back in style, and three storm windows that evidently belong to another house.

When it came right down to it, though, there was nothing to making that costume. By giving up lunch I whipped the whole thing up in less than a month. And finally the day arrived. Johnny was a superb Frosty. His was an exquisitely conceived, finely wrought performance—limpid, luminous, tender. When he took his bows there was tremendous applause, in which he enthusiastically joined. I could just hear him in Congress, forty years from now, referring to himself as "the able Senator from New York."

This production ended, however, in a short tableau that said to me that the day of economy and sincerity was not wholly past. A small redheaded boy in a brown toga, with dirty sneakers showing briefly beneath, escorted a tiny girl in white dress and blue veil across the stage. He stopped suddenly and said, in a voice of piercing sweetness:

"Oh, Mary, 'tis a cold, cold night."

Mary turned and said simply: " 'Tis."

It won't make a nickel, but it's a great audience show.

12. How to get the best of your children

WHEN I SEE lists of the great women of history, I always want to add the name of a woman who was a neighbor of mine in Washington. She crept into my heart forever one very hot day when, as I was passing directly under her window, I heard her say, in a quiet, musical voice, "Michael dear, Mommy doesn't *like* you to drive your bicycle into the piano."

That's character. That's forbearance. Now if it had been *my* piano and *my* Michael—well, we won't go into that, there's too much senseless violence in print already. But here we get to the nub of the problem.

The Everest of my ambition is to teach my children the simple precepts of existence—"Keep your fingers out of the plate," "Don't wear your underwear to bed," "Keep out of Federal institutions"—and somehow arrive at golden middle age with my larynx intact.

No matter how I struggle to keep my voice out of that piercing upper register where, I am told, only dogs can hear it, my boys can always discover the one little chink in my armor of control. For instance, when it is my turn to get them up in the morning, I spring down the stairs (after three hours' sleep), jaunty and adorable in my husband's old dressing gown.

I brace myself against the dazzling sight of all those eager, ill-scrubbed faces. I tell myself that it is quite natural for children to be cheerful at seven o'clock in the morning. I further resolve that I am going to remain calm. Calm, do you hear—*calm*. As I see it, I'm not strong and I owe it to myself to maintain peace and—this is laughable—quiet. Discipline can come later when we are all up to it.

So I find three lost shoes, put a new cover on Colin's speller, comb the entire house for thirty-two cents milk money, and untie Gilbert, who has been strapped to a chair with a cowboy belt while I was looking for the money. All this while I'm exuding such syrupy good cheer that the children are downright awed. I hear myself saying, in the cool, improbable tones of Betty Furness discussing a new icebox, "Just because he ate your crayons is no reason to hit him on the head with a coke bottle."

When they are finally seated at breakfast, I watch the twins spell out their names in butter on the plastic place mats—but I refuse to get riled. When they all decide to make sandwiches of boiled egg and puffed wheat, I remind myself that after all they're just Little Boys and we can cope with this sometime in the future.

Then I notice Christopher stirring his orange juice with an old pocket comb. At this point everything snaps and my wild, sweet soprano can be heard in Mamaroneck.

When I was younger and full of Dr. Spock I used to make the common mistake of trying to be "fair" with the children. At the peak of every crisis I would summon the entire brood from the four corners of the television set and ask stern, equivocal questions like "Who threw the calendar in the toilet?" Naturally, nobody did.

Now I rely on blind instinct. After assessing the evidence and asking myself a few routine questions like who was in the bathroom last and who is sopping wet, I seize the probable culprit, give him a little whack, and announce flatly, "*So*, you threw the calendar in the toilet!"

The real menace in dealing with a five-year old is that in no
time at all you begin to sound like a five-year old.

This undoubtedly leads to an occasional injustice, but you'd be surprised how it cuts down on the plumbing bills.

Another distressing aspect of disciplining young children is that somehow you are always left with the flat end of the dialogue—a straight man forever. It's not just that you *feel* idiotic. The real menace in dealing with a five-year-old is that in no time at all you begin to sound like a five-year-old. Let's say you hear a loud, horrifying crash from the bedroom, so you shout up:

"In heaven's name, what was that?"

"What?"

"That awful noise."

"What noise?"

"You didn't hear that noise?"

"No. Did you?"

"Of course I did—I just told you."

"What did it sound like?"

"Never mind what it sounded like. Just stop it."

"Stop what?"

"Whatever you're doing."

"I'm not doing anything."

"Stop it anyway!"

"I'm brushing my teeth. Shall I stop that?"

Obviously, this way lies madness. Personally, I knew I had to win this battle of dialectics or seek psychiatric care. I don't promise that my solution will work equally well in all cases, but it does nicely around here. Nowadays when I hear that crash I merely call up, clearly and firmly, "Hey you, pick up your pants."

I am, of course, operating on the absolute certainty that whoever it is will have at least one pair of pants on the floor. And the mere motion of picking them up will distract him, temporarily at least, from whatever mayhem he was involved in. As far as that crash is concerned, I never *really* wanted to know what it was. I just wanted it to *stop*.

Incidentally, the worst thing you can do when reprimanding children is to indicate the nature and the degree of your desperation. For instance, you accomplish nothing by throwing yourself on their mercy and asking piteously, "Are you trying to drive your poor mommy smack out of her mind?" Of course they are, but do you think they'll admit it?

I find among my friends many examples of the insecure or "hit-and-run" type of disciplinarian. Little Kathie has deliberately thrown an unopened can of evaporated milk at Mother's ear. So Mother responds by spanking Kathie's behind with a bedroom slipper. (These are excellent for the purpose because, while the noise produced is awesome, the damage is negligible.) However, at the first sign of that golden tear trickling down Kathie's cute little nose, Mother melts, clasps the little fiend to her breast, and murmurs, "Mommy didn't mean it, Mommy's a mean, mean mommy." And so forth.

I will admit that on one notable occasion I had to fight against that impulse myself. When the children were really small we had a little game. I would say, "Are you my friend?" And they would answer "I'm your good, *true* friend."

Well, one night when the twins were about three I deposited the two of them in the bathtub while I put the baby to bed. As I was changing the baby on his table, I could hear the sloshing and splashing of what appeared to be an Aquacade in high gear. I called in several times, warning them to stop all the horsing around. Eventually I had to dump the baby in the crib and dash into the bathroom, where I smacked every fanny that was available (and you'd be astounded at how many fannies a pair of twins seem to have).

Then, as I beat my retreat back to the bedroom, there was an eerie silence—broken at last by Johnny, who announced in cold, sinister tones, "Well, she's just lost two good, true friends."

I confess that the enormity of my loss did give me pause. I was unnerved for days.

Even at that, the pangs you get after you punish

children are nothing compared to the problems that arise *before* you punish them. One day recently, after Christopher had left for school, I discovered that he had used my brand-new lipstick to draw a pirate's treasure map on the floor of the garage. I was just waiting to get my hands on him when he arrived at four o'clock, all smiles and snatches of song.

And I was just starting to call to him when I heard him ask his father, "Hi, Dad, where is La Belle Señorita?"

Now what do you do in a case like that? Damned if I know.

13. Where did you put the aspirin?

I'D BE THE LAST one to say a word against our modern child psychologists. They try, they really try. I know that. So I am prepared to swallow a number of their curious notions, including even the thought-provoking statement that "children are our Friends." This premise may be open to question, or even to hysterical laughter, but it probably does contain a germ of truth.

What I have no patience with is the growing tendency among psychologists to insist that children are really *people*, little adults—just like the rest of us, only smaller. Really, the impression you get in some quarters is that the only difference between children and grownups is that children don't drink, smoke, or play bridge.

Come, come, men. We all know better than that. Children are different—mentally, physically, spiritually, quantitatively, qualitatively, and furthermore they're all a little bit nuts.

Take a simple matter like going to bed. An adult will say, "If *you* want to sit up all night watching an old George Raft movie, okay, but I'm turning in." And he turns in, and that's the end of him until tomorrow morning.

Getting a child to bed is a different proposition altogether. First you locate your child and make a simple

announcement to the effect that it is now bedtime. This
leads to a spirited debate in which you have to listen
to a passionate defense of the many mothers of character and vision who live just up the block and who
always allow their seven-year-old boys to stay up and
watch Bilko. (Indeed, if my informant is correct, ours
are the only children in Larchmont who don't habitually
sit up to catch *Night Beat*.)

You gently and gracefully present your side of the
picture. "Listen," you say, "I don't want to hear one
more word about Rory Killilea's mother. You're going
to bed right now, do you hear, *now*, this minute!"
These persuasive remarks, declaimed in clear, ringing
tones with perhaps an additional "This Minute!"
thrown in for good measure, are usually sufficient to
get a boy up into the bedroom. Theoretically, the matter
is closed. Actually, you've just begun to fight.

Now begins a series of protracted farewell appearances. He comes back on the landing to say that his
pajamas are wet and he has a neat idea: he's going to
sleep in his snow pants. You say it's impossible, how
could those pajamas be wet? And he says he doesn't
know unless it's because he used them to mop up the
floor when he tipped over the fish tank.

It shouldn't take you more than fifteen minutes to
find his other pajamas—the ones that haven't got any
buttons, the ones that are supposed to be in the clean-
clothes hamper but aren't. When you've finally got
him pinned into that dry pair, you can go back and
glare at your husband, who has found the whole inci-
dent rather amusing (well, dammit, he's a *boy*). Your
husband's hilarity, however, will be somewhat quenched
in a moment when he hears that one of the fish has
perished in the disaster and will require an immediate
burial outside by flashlight.

But soft! That boy is back again, and we are into the
following dialogue:

"I suppose you want me to brush my teeth."

"Of course I want you to brush your teeth."

Now begins a series of protracted farewell appearances.

"Okay, but I won't be going to school tomorrow."

"Why not, for heaven's sake?"

"Because I'll be poisoned to death."

"What *are* you talking about?"

"Chris used my toothbrush to paint his model car."

This necessitates a brief but painful interview with Chris, who declares, "He never used that toothbrush anyway, he always used mine."

Normally, along about here, you can count on a seven-minute *Luftpause* during which you can cut out a recipe for Baked Alaska which you will make as soon as you lose ten pounds, which will be never.

But we're about ready for that third appearance. "Mommy"—this time the voice is dripping with tragedy —"Mommy, it's raining."

You leap out of your chair.

"Do you mean to tell me that you got up just to tell me it's raining? I *know* it's raining. Go back to bed!"

He goes back, but presently the sound of muffled sobs come flooding down the stair well. Naturally, you have to go upstairs and turn on the light and find out what's the matter with the poor little thing. What's the matter, it turns out, is that he has left his bicycle over on the Slezaks' lawn. Not that he is at all concerned about the bicycle, which he has just got for Christmas and which cost thirty-nine dollars and ninety-five cents, but he has tied a keen foxtail to the handle bar and it will be ruined, just absolutely ruined. So you can go over and get the bicycle and if you hurry you'll be back in time to catch his fourth and final appearance.

This time, noticing the edge of hysteria in your voice (he's been around for seven years; he knows when you are going to crack), he keeps his message brief.

"Mommy, this is important. I have to have a costume for the play tomorrow. I'm Saint Joseph."

If children and adults differ in their approach to bedtime, there is even greater discrepancy in the separate ways they greet the morn. To begin with, the average, healthy, well-adjusted adult gets up at seven-thirty in the morning feeling just plain terrible. He stumbles through the physical motions of dressing, staring glassily at the shirt button that has just come off in his hand. His mind, oddly enough, is razor-sharp, probing, questioning: why was he born, why are there never any clean handkerchiefs, where will all this end? He's moody, morose, and above all else—silent. (This is a desirable situation, since it makes it easier for him to live with that other healthy, normal adult who isn't feeling so top-of-the-morning either.) He walks with a slight list, holding his hands out in front of him—presumably to catch his head should it fall off. During the entire breakfast period he will break the silence only once, to mutter hoarsely, "*I* don't call this *half* the paper, this is nothing but real estate ads."

Now we come to the little ones, who rise from their beds like a swarm of helicopters buzzing and sawing the air around them. Although it's only seven-thirty, they haven't been idle. One of them has written "I am a pig" on the bathroom mirror with tooth paste—and won't that be a cool joke on Gilbert when he is old enough to read? Somebody else has found a good secret hiding place for his pirate knife: he just cut a little corner off the pillow and stuffed it inside, and *that* clears up the mystery of where all those feathers came from. Even so, it's not the mayhem that eats away at the nerve ends of the adult; it is the riotous good humor and wild, gay chatter that spills like a Kansas twister out of the bedroom, down the stairs, and over the breakfast table.

If the matutinal conversation of children and grown-ups differs in volume and velocity, it also differs in essence. An adult, if he speaks at all, makes statements ("Well, I see Walter Lippmann is after Dulles again"), a remark that not only doesn't require an answer, it practically precludes one.

The child, on the other hand, makes questions. Even when he is only trying to impart information, he will phrase it as a query: "Did you know that the Egyp-

tians invented marshmallow?" "Did you know that
Billy said if his turtle has a turtle he's going to give
me a turtle?"

Now, most of these questions can be answered by a
simple "Yep." (This is clearly not the time to give
your reasons for supposing that the output of a solitary
turtle will be necessarily limited.) There is a danger,
though, that you will "yep" your way into trouble by
missing the ghastly implications of a trick question like,
"Do you want to see me drink my milk without touching
the glass with my hands?"

There are other important ways in which children
differ from their elders. For instance, it is perfectly
possible to have a really satisfactory quarrel with an
adult. You say to the beloved, "Do you mean to tell
me that you met Mrs. Gordon and you didn't ask her
about her operation? Of *course* I told you, you just
don't *listen*. Oh, never mind—you're obtuse, that's all,
just plain *thick!*" This should lead to a spirited ex-
change and result in a good, two-day sulk.

Conversely, you can tell a child that he's the worst
boy ever born into the world, follow up this sweeping statement with a smart thump on the behind, and in
two and one half minutes he will come back, look you
straight in the eye, and say, "Wanna hear a neat
riddle?"

Of course we haven't time here to discuss the more
obvious and basic differences, such as the fact that
adults believe in Santa Claus and children don't. But
we must get in a word about the Sweater Fetish that
is so peculiar to the young. Adults, many of them,
don't *have* sweaters, and those who do find that the
mere possession of a sweater in no way detracts from
their enjoyment of a rich, full life. Children, however,
regard the Sweater primarily as something to take off.
More than that. They see in the Sweater a symbol of
all that is plainly idiotic and unreasonable about the
adult world. I'm sure that even in Alaska, when the
temperature thuds to fifty below zero, little Eskimo

children plead, "Do I *have* to wear it? It's not cold."
To me, there is something almost touching about the
way children fight the daily, doomed battle of the
Sweater. It's as though they were saying to themselves, "Okay, I have to wear this, but someday, somewhere, some kid who is bigger than me and better than
me is going to make it out that back door without one."
There are, to be sure, some lucky childern who *don't*
have sweaters, having left them in school, or in the
park or in a drawer wrapped around a pair of ice
skates.

Psychologists tell us that the things we *want,* the
things we ask for most often, provide us with a vital
clue to our personalities. Children, having linear minds
and no grasp of the great intangibles, spend most of
their energy yapping about trifles: "Can I have a
Coke?" "Can I have an apple?" "Can I have a Good
Humor?" "Can I see *Baby Doll?* Dickie says it's a keen
picture."

In contrast, notice the maturity and breadth of vision
that is revealed in this sampling of a typical adult's
daily demands: "Where did you put the aspirin?"
"Did anybody call the plumber about that faucet?"
"Don't you *ever* put cigarettes out?" "Tell them we
can't come, tell them I'm sick, tell them I'm dead, tell
them anything you want!" "Who the hell took my
fountain pen?"

Let's have no more of this nonsense about children
being Little Adults. They are a breed apart, and you
can tell it just by looking at them. How many of them
have gray hair? How many do you see taking Miltown?
How many go to psychiatrists?

Okay, we've settled that.

14. Aunt Jean's marshmallow fudge diet

FRED ALLEN used to talk about a man who was so thin he could be dropped through a piccolo without striking a single note. Well, I'm glad I never met *him;* I'd hate to have to hear about *his* diet.

I can remember when I was a girl—way back in Truman's administration—and No-Cal was only a gleam in the eye of the Hirsch Bottling Company. In those days it was fun to go to parties. The conversation used to crackle with wit and intelligence because we talked about *ideas*—the esthetic continuum in western culture, Gary Cooper in western movies, the superiority of beer over lotion as a wave-set, and the best way to use leftover veal.

Go to a party now and the couple next to you won't say a word about the rich, chocolate texture of their compost heap or how practical it's been to buy bunk beds for the twins. They won't talk about anything whatsoever except their diets—the one they've just come off, the one they're on now, or the one they're going to have to start on Monday if they keep lapping it up like this.

I really blame science for the whole business. Years ago when a man began to notice that if he stood up on

Aunt Jean's marshmallow fudge diet.

the subway he was immediately replaced by *two* people, he figured he was getting too fat. So he went to his doctor and the doctor said, "Quit stuffing yourself, Joe." And Joe either stopped or he didn't stop, but at least he kept his big mouth shut about the whole matter. What was there to talk about?

Today, with the science of nutrition advancing so rapidly, there is plenty of food for conversation, if for nothing else. We have the Rockefeller diet, the Mayo diet, high-protein diets, low-protein diets, "blitz" diets which feature cottage cheese and something that tastes like very thin sandpaper, and—finally—a liquid diet that duplicates all the rich, nourishing goodness of mother's milk. I have no way of knowing which of these is the most efficacious for losing weight, but there's no question in my mind that as a conversation-stopper the "mother's milk diet" is quite a ways out ahead.

Where do people get all these diets, anyway? Obviously from the magazines; it's impossible to get a diet from a newspaper. For one thing, in a newspaper you can never catch the diet when it *starts*. It's always the fourth day of Ada May's Wonder Diet and, after a brief description of a simple slimming exercise that could be performed by anybody who has had five years' training with the ballet, Ada May gives you the menu for the day. One glass of skim milk, eight prunes, and three lamb kidneys. This settles the matter for most people, who figure —quite reasonably—that if this is the *fourth* day, heaven deliver them from the first.

However, any stoics in the group who want to know just how far Ada May's sense of whimsey will take her can have the complete diet by sending twenty-five cents in stamps to the newspaper. But there you are. Who has twenty-five cents in stamps? You're not running a branch of the post office. And if you're going to go out and get the stamps you might as well buy a twenty-five-cent magazine which will give you not only the same diet (now referred to as *Our* Wonder Diet) but will, in addition, show you a quick and easy way to turn your husband's old socks into gay pot holders.

In a truly democratic magazine that looks at all sides of the picture you will also find a recipe for George Washington's favorite spice cake, which will replace any weight you may have haphazardly lost on that wonder diet.

If you have formed the habit of checking on every *new* diet that comes along, you will find that, mercifully, they all blur together, leaving you with only one definite piece of information: french-fried potatoes are out. But once in a great while a diet will stick in your mind. I'll never forget one I read about last summer. It urged the dieter to follow up his low-calorie meals by performing a series of calisthenics in the bathtub. No, not in the bath*room*. I read it twice, and it said in the bath*tub*. What a clever plan! Clearly, after you've broken both your arms you won't be able to eat much (if at all) and the pounds will just melt away. In fact, if you don't have a co-operative husband who is willing to feed you like a two-year-old you may be limited to what you can consume through a straw, in which case let me suggest that mother's milk formula diet.

The best diet I've heard about lately is the simplest. It was perfected by the actor Walter Slezak after years of careful experimentation. Under the Slezak plan, you eat as much as you want of everything you don't like. And if you should be in a hurry for any reason (let's say you're still wearing maternity clothes and the baby is eight months old), then you should confine yourself to food that you just plain hate.

Speaking about hateful food, the experts used to be content with merely making food pallid—by eliminating butter, oil, and salt. Not any more. Nowadays we are taught that, with a little imagination and a judicious use of herbs, anyone can turn out a no-calorie dish that's downright ghastly. Just yesterday I came across a dandy recipe for sprucing up good old boiled celery. You just simmer the chopped celery (with the tops) in a little skim milk. When it's tender, you add chopped onion, anise, chervil, marjoram, a dash of cinnamon, and you have a dish fit for the Dispose-All. And you'd better have a Dispose-All, because it's awfully messy if you have to dump it into a newspaper and carry it out to the garbage can.

And where is all this dieting getting us? No place at all. It's taken all the fun out of conversation and all the joy out of cooking. Furthermore, it leads to acts of irrational violence. A friend of mine keeps all candy and other luscious tidbits in the freezer, on the theory that by the time they thaw out enough to be eaten she will have recovered her will power. But the other night, having been driven berserk by a four-color advertisement for Instant Brownies, she rushed out to the freezer, started to gnaw on a frozen Milky Way, and broke off her front tooth.

But let's get to the heart of the matter. All these diets that appear so monotonously in the flossy magazines—who are they for? Are they aimed at men? Certainly not; most men don't read these magazines. Are they intended for fat teen-agers? Probably not; teen-agers can't afford them. Do not ask for whom the bell tolls. It tolls for you, Married Woman, Mother of Three, lumpy, dumpy, and the source of concern to practically every publication in the country. And why, why is the married woman being hounded into starvation in order to duplicate an ideal figure which is neither practical nor possible for a person her age? I'll tell you why.

First, it is presumed that when you're thinner you live longer. (In any case, when you live on a diet of yogurt and boiled grapefruit, it *seems* longer.) Second, it is felt that when you are skin and bones you have so much extra energy that you can climb up and shingle the roof. Third—and this is what they're really getting at—when you're thin you are so tasty and desirable that strange men will pinch you at the A & P and your husband will not only follow you around the kitchen breathing heavily but will stop and smother you with

I have taken a cross section of the divorcees.

kisses as you try to put the butter back in the icebox. This—and I hope those in the back of the room are listening—is hogwash.

Think of the happy marriages you know about. How many of the ladies are still wearing size twelve? I've been giving this a lot of thought in the last twenty minutes, and I have been examining the marriages in my own troubled circle. More than that, I have taken a cross section of the divorcees. (Cross? My dear, they were irate!) What I have discovered—attention, Beauty Editors everywhere!—is that the women who are being ditched are one and all willowy, wand-like, and slim as a blade. In fact, six of them require extensive padding even to look flat-chested.

That the fourteen divorcees, or about-to-be divorcees, whom I happen to know personally are thin may be nothing more than a coincidence. Or it may just prove that men don't divorce fat wives because they feel sorry for them. Then again—and this is rather sinister—men may not divorce fat wives because they imagine that the poor, plump dears will never locate *another* husband and they'll be paying alimony to the end of their days. (I mention this possibility, but my heart's not in it.)

The real reason, I believe, that men hang onto their well-endowed spouses is because they're comfy and nice to have around the house. In a marriage there is nothing that stales so fast as physical beauty—as we readers of *Modern Screen* have observed. What actually holds a husband through thick and thick is a girl who is fun to be with. And any girl who has had nothing to eat since nine o'clock this morning but three hard-boiled eggs will be about as jolly and companionable as an income-tax inspector.

So I say, ladies, find out why women everywhere are switching from old-fashioned diets to the *modern* way: no exercise, no dangerous drugs, no weight loss. (And what do they mean, "ugly fat"? It's *you*, isn't it?) For that tired, run-down feeling, try eating three full meals a day with a candy bar after dinner and pizza at eleven o'clock. Don't be intimidated by pictures of Audrey Hepburn. That girl is nothing but skin and bones. Just sit there smiling on that size-twenty backside and say, "Guess what we're having for dinner, dear? Your favorite—stuffed breast of veal and corn fritters." All of your friends will say, "Oh, Blanche is a mess, the size of a house, but he's crazy about her, just *crazy* about her!"

15. Operation operation

OBVIOUSLY this is not the moment to be talking about operations when here we all are—in the very bloom of health. But these are troubled times, and there are people in St. Vincent's Hospital today who, as recently as yesterday, didn't know they *had* a spinal disk. The thing to do, I say, is be prepared, bone up, get the facts so that your stay in the hospital will be the jolly, satisfying interlude it ought to be.

I don't know whether or not I am speaking for convalescents everywhere, but I can tell you that *my* big mistake when I go to the hospital is being too cheerful. I arrive the day before the operation and, while it would be stretching things to suggest that on this occasion I feel fit, I at least feel human. So I try to be agreeable. Agreeable nothing; I'm adorable to a point just short of nausea. With my gay sayings and my air of quiet self-deprecation, I creep into the heart of one and all.

"Yes," I murmur to the night nurse, "I did ring for you an hour ago, but that's *perfectly* all right." And I reassure the orderly who forgot to bring my dinner tray with a blithe "Don't worry about it, I'm not the least bit hungry and besides I have these delicious cherry cough drops."

But then the morrow comes, and with it my opera-

135

—my big mistake—is being too cheerful.

tion. As I'm wheeled back from the Recovery Room it becomes absolutely clear that, while the operation was a great success, I am a total failure. I feel completely, utterly, unspeakably miserable, and I see no reason why any member of the staff should be kept in ignorance of this sorry state of affairs. I ring bells, buzz buzzers, snap at nurses, and generally behave in a manner that can best be described as loathsome.

Of course, the nurses have seen post-operative cases before, but clearly they expected more of *me*. It's as though June Allyson had been transformed into Ana Pauker right before their eyes. And they feel, not unreasonably, that they have been betrayed. As a result, the whole staff gives me approximately the same brisk, gingerly attention they would bestow on an old bandage. Even at the end of the fourth day—when I'm once again feeling pro-social and want to kiss and make up—they will have none of me.

The best solution to this problem, short of being a good little soldier all the time, is to be a teeny bit curt when you first arrive. Don't pose as an Eva Marie Saint. Show your true colors. Keep your tone brisk. Then there will be no unpleasant shocks later.

And there are other steps you can take. Actually, to cope with ordinary hospital routine you really ought to be in good physical condition. Since this is hardly practical—you wouldn't be in the hospital if you were in good physical condition—you can do the best thing: be mentally alert, be systematic. Remember: if they have rules, *you* have rules.

Rule One: *Refuse to be bullied.* It is the the custom in most hospitals for the night nurse to wake all her patients before she goes off duty at six o'clock in the morning and present each of them with a basin of lukewarm water and a bar of soap. Then, a few seconds later, the incoming day nurse rushes in and takes everybody's temperature. This is a very sensible procedure because most people say they notice a very definite rise in temperature (together with a tendency to break down and sob) merely at being required to *look* at a basin of water at six o'clock in the morning, and the day nurse now has something concrete to put on her chart. She doesn't have to feel a failure.

How do you eliminate this dawn patrol? It's no use complaining to the nurse; she's met your type before. Any piteous explanations on your part like, "Nurse, please, I haven't been to sleep at all, they just gave me a sedative half an hour ago and besides I'm clean, look, *clean!*" will only confirm her growing suspicion that you have no team spirit and, what's worse, no regard at all for personal daintiness.

After much trial and error I have worked out a rather neat little system for beating this game. I simply explain to the nurse that I am undergoing psychoanalysis for an old guilt trauma which dates back to the time when I was three years old and shoved my little sister into a golf bag. Ever since, I tell her, I've shown manifestations of the Lady Macbeth complex, an aberration in which the victim has a continuous and compulsive desire to wash her hands. Consequently, as a part of my therapy I am forbidden by my analyst to wash more than three times a day.

I am also working on a plan—it's unfortunately still in the blueprint stage—that would limit the number of times a nurse took your temperature to something reasonable, say eight or nine times in a single afternoon. At that, it's not really the frequency that's so maddening, it's the duration. What do you suppose there is in the Nightingale code that impels a nurse to put a thermometer in somebody's mouth just before she goes off to assist at an appendectomy? There you are, left like a beached submarine with this little periscope poking from your mouth while all about you life goes on, children are born, and you who have so much to contribute can do nothing but nibble on that damn little glass tube.

I just take it out the minute her back is turned and carefully replace it about five minutes before she returns. There's no real risk of detection, because a truly conscientious nurse will always stop off at the linen closet on her way back and her approach will be heralded by the snatches of fascinating dialogue that float down the corridors:

"Listen, fourteen needs a top sheet."

"Nonsense, I gave fourteen two sheets yesterday."

"Okay, you tell that to fourteen."

The system is practically foolproof.

Rule Two: *Act your age.* One of the most difficult things to contend with in a hospital is the assumption on the part of the staff that because you have lost your gall bladder you have also lost your mind. Personally, I find it rather piquant to be treated like a four-year-old. ("Are we feeling any better? Shall we sit up and eat our nice lunch?") The only objectionable aspect of this constant use of the plural is that it leaves me with the feeling that I'm *two* four-year-olds.

And you do have to say one thing for these cuddly, nursy-knows-best disciplinarians: they're loyal, they complete the task assigned. Neither storm nor sleet nor gloom of night will stay them from the swift completion of their appointed rounds. This was brought home to me in a very real way during my last sojourn in the hospital when a dear little night nurse woke me from a sound sleep to give me a sleeping pill. Sometimes this business of hewing to the narrow line of duty produces results bordering on the miraculous. A writer I once heard about flew to Evanston to visit his eighty-year-old mother who had just had an operation. Arriving, he met a nurse in the corridor, asked for a report on the patient, and was told that she had made all the routine objections to being put on her feet five days after the operation but that the staff had been firm, quite firm, and now the old lady was trotting around like everybody else. The writer was deeply impressed. "Good Lord," he said, "she hasn't walked in five years."

You see the point, don't you? If the lady in question

had stood on her rights as an eighty-year-old, she'd still be sitting pretty in that rocking chair, where she wanted to be.

Rule Three: *Get the facts*. It seems to me that too many people accept hospital routine with cowlike apathy, whereas a little intellectual curiosity would be broadening to the patient and stimulating to the staff. Let's say that two interns approach you with a cartful of sinister-looking tubes and announce casually, "We're going to give you a Harris Flush."

Don't just lie there. Get the whole story. Who was Harris? What is this flush? When did Harris get the idea in the first place? Whatever happened to Harris?

Why shouldn't you ask a question from time to time? It's only quid pro quo. From the moment you get into that hospital coat and they lock away your shoes, there is a constant parade of cheery interns, all of them popping with more questions than Mary Margaret McBride. What was your mother's maiden name? Did you ever have any broken limbs? How old were you when you had chicken pox? If there is anything more striking than their fascination with that attack of measles you had in 1927, it's their total disinterest in that ruptured appendix which explains your presence here at this moment.

My father spent some time in a hospital a couple of years ago, and he began by being very patient and co-operative about answering all the routine questions. At the end of an hour's inquisition the intern asked him how old *his* father was when he died. Dad explained, with pardonable pride, that his father had died at the age of ninety-five. The intern looked up from his notes and inquired, with the air of one about to make a significant discovery, "What did he die of?" Whereupon my father exploded. "My God, man, he died because he was *ninety-five!*"

While interns may be lacking in other qualities, I want no one to tell me that they don't have a sense of humor. At first glance, this sense of humor may seem

—there is a constant parade of interns, all of them
popping with questions . . .

to be a trifle macabre. Actually, it fits perfectly into the cold, brilliant tradition of Ben Jonson, Dean Swift, and Charles Addams. Why else would an intern deposit a patient due for an eight-o'clock operation outside the operating-room door at seven-thirty, where she will be in a position to overhear the highlights of the preceding operation?

You can picture the scene, can't you? There is the patient, strapped to a cart, partially sedated, and feeling a good deal less than hearty. And through the transom comes a rough male voice saying, "Boy, I never thought it would spurt like *that*." Oh, there's no end to the possibilities for good, clean, sinister mirth.

Rule Four: *Look the part*. Let's not pretend that all the mistakes made in hospitals are made by the staff. I've known patients who have made beauts. As far as I'm concerned, there is nothing more idiotic than the spectacle of a woman just coming out of ether who immediately struggles into a fluffy pink bed jacket and ties a tender blue ribbon into her limp curls. Though scarcely able to lift an arm, she somehow succeeds in applying two layers of make-up before the stroke of visiting hour.

What happens? Gay husband arrives, bearing an azalea, and announces, "Boy, honey, *you* look great, but let me tell you about the day I had!"

My own theory, which owes something—at least in spirit—to T. S. Eliot's principle of the "objective correlative," can be stated simply: if you feel terrible, look terrible. Save that blue ribbon until the happy moment arrives when you notice that you can comb even the back of your hair without becoming so faint that you have to lie down for half an hour afterwards. In addition to the fact that by simulating recovery you get none of the sympathy which psychologists tell us is so necessary in convalescence, you run the further risk of being brought home from the hospital prematurely. There you'll be, back in the kitchen frying pork chops, when everybody knows you need rest, rest, rest. So I say: no lipstick, forget about the cold cream, *let* those fine lines appear. Make it very difficult for your friends to tell you that they never saw you looking better in your life. With any luck, you may even startle an acquaintance into making an intelligent remark, like "Helen, you poor darling, you look ghastly—I bet you feel rotten, don't you?"

Rule Five: I'm sorry, but Rule Five seems to have gone out of my head. I have this sharp pain. Well, it's more like a twinge than a pain—but a *deep* twinge. Excuse me while I call Dr. Meredith.

FREE
Fawcett Books Listing

There is Romance, Mystery, Suspense, and Adventure waiting for you inside the Fawcett Books Order Form. And it's yours to browse through and use to get all the books you've been wanting . . . but possibly couldn't find in your bookstore.

This easy-to-use order form is divided into categories and contains over 1500 titles by your favorite authors.

So don't delay—take advantage of this special opportunity to increase your reading pleasure.

Just send us your name and address and 35¢ (to help defray postage and handling costs).